In Medias Res

In Medias Res

Laura Hewett

Copyright © 2025 by Laura Hewett
All rights reserved. No part of this book may be reproduced in any manner whatsoever without written permission except in the case of brief quotations embodied in critical articles and reviews. No permission is given to use any portion of this material for AI training.
First Printing, 2025

CONTENTS

Introduction	1
1	Thoughts at Ten Years	3
In Medias Res	10
2	On Pain	12
3	On Depression	27
4	On Dying	43
Extra Auntie	54
5	On Moving	55
6	On Hospitality	69
7	On Community	81
A Note on Tenses	91
8	On Teaching	92
9	On Learning	109
10	On Graduation	121
When It's October Again	135
11	On Following	137

12 On Stories 147
13 On Prayer 156
   Loose Ends 174

ACKNOWLEDGEMENTS 175

Introduction

I broke my back, and it dramatically shifted the trajectory of my life.

In some ways.

In others, I'm very much who I was always going to be, who I had begun to become before the moment concrete collided with my bum and broke my L3 and L1 vertebrae.

Early on, a friend encouraged me to write my story. She believed it would be different written at year three than at year seventeen or something like that. Well, I wrote a full draft of a memoir in year five post-disability. I sat with it for a few years and published a couple of other things before coming back after my tenth traumaversary to revisit, revise, and recount some significant lessons and insights from the whole scope of my life — before and after the accident.

I grew up a relatively healthy and asthmatic kid in a caring home with two Jesus loving parents and a brainiac older sister to keep up with. My parents had moved with their tiny firstborn from Colorado to Oregon a couple of years before I was born. I'd never lived outside the suburbs of Portland all the way until I graduated with my Masters in Teaching and accepted a job at Black Forest Academy (BFA) in Kandern, Germany. Moving there was where I learned about the whole world of TCKs, or Third Culture Kids, a unique demographic of people who spent a significant portion of their formative years in a culture different than their passport. My spinal cord injury happened the first year I moved to Germany, but I loved my job and chose to stay much longer than my initial two year commitment. After five years, I was required to leave for 366 days for a "totalisation period" according to the visa agreements related to social security between my host and passport countries. I spent the majority of that time on sabbatical volunteering at Riccarton Community Church (RCC) in Christchurch, New Zealand before returning to BFA for four more years. After ending my time at BFA, I took a job on staff at RCC and returned to New Zealand long term.

As I recount my story here, there's some obvious discussion on spinal cord injury and the rather significant trauma of breaking my back in a rock climbing facility. Most of that is focused in the "On Pain" chapter. The following chapter, "On Depression," recounts stories of several people with past and present battles of suicide ideation. "On Dying" includes reflections on grief, death, and gun violence. I've included these hard topics because they are relevant to my story, and I invite you to read with whatever sensitivity you need to bring from your own story.

The first draft of this memoir was a collection of twelve chapters, each with thoughts on a particular topic, a relevant life story before my accident, and a story with a different student I met after my accident. Most of those chapters remain relatively intact; others were removed or adjusted as I freed myself from that structure. Another significant change in my life since the initial draft of this text is that I started writing poetry again. I used to write terrible angsty stuff in high school which I laid aside until the summer of 2020. Some really wild non-corona related things happened in my life that summer, and prose temporarily failed me. I interspersed a couple of poems as fitting into this revised draft. Notably, here, I invite you into the middle of my story. I'm publishing this over ten years after my accident, but who knows how many years and adventures lay ahead. I can only tell you that you met me in the middle of my story, or as literature teachers might say, you met me "in medias res."

1

Thoughts at Ten Years

Every spinal cord injury is different. That's what the doctors, nurses, occupational therapists, and physios all emphasised to me in the hospital all those years ago. There were best guesses and prognosis predictions, but everything was given with the caveat that the experts didn't really know how much I would recover. When I met Frau Dr. Hound, the head of the REHAB Basel facility for the first time, I asked a naive question about whether I'd ever walk again. "Let's see if you can ever stand again," came the honest Swiss response. She didn't know that I'd already stood with support from the physios in my laborious physical therapy sessions. Little did she know I'd write this from my standing desk ten years later (I didn't know that part either). She was just like Frau Dr. Netzer, my talented Swiss surgeon. Dr. Netzer's first conversation with me included the sentence, "I make no promises of you ever walking again," and she was shocked when I walked into her office a year later with the help of four-footed canes and ankle-foot orthotics. I've been defying medical professionals for the past decade. Even Mike, the Kiwi physio I spent my sabbatical working with, told me I broke all the rules for nerve damage. The Aussie team of specialists who do exercise based rehab with spinal cord patients weren't surprised by my abilities or limits — because they knew the same mantra that every spinal cord injury is different.

When I broke my back ten years ago, I had thousands of people around the world hear about my accident and begin praying for me. Hundreds dropped off the prayer team within a few weeks. Plenty more stayed faithful in their petitions to God, but that eventually tapered off over time.

Then new people joined the story for either short bursts or long haul commitments to pray for my ongoing growth and recovery. Even with people who were only in my story for a chapter or a season, I'm so grateful for the touchpoint and opportunity to connect with other people interested in my healing journey. The ten year mark brought a lot of new people into my story, and was worth the time to reflect well on a decade of holistic healing.

Sure, all those physical implications seem like a good lead in, but it's not the most interesting part of my story. I get a lot of initial attention because of the wheelchair. However, what I've realised is that when I'm able to hold interest from others, it's got nothing to do with my disability. This isn't like a toxic positivity thing either. Certainly there are silver linings to my disability, and you'll absolutely see me highlight them, but you'll hopefully not ignore the glaring, bold print moments of how **disability sucks**. Spinal cord injuries are traumatic and unpleasant and have horrible long-term consequences. Cutting in line at the airport isn't worth it for the hassle of strategic dehydration and anxiety over possibly losing parts of my wheelchair due to careless employees throwing cargo into the plane.

I once reflected with a former student during a moment of grief in his life about how he could share the happiness of his friend. My exact words sent in a message to him were, "You can also hold the joy of others as distinct from your emotions. Put their happiness in one hand that you offer to them and hold your grief in the other that you share with someone else later." This is a really important life lesson. I sent that message the week one of my students who I was particularly close to passed away unexpectedly. I was an absolute mess that week, but I had other people who didn't know my grief who wanted to share their joy with me. I've gone back to that concept time and time again with relationship to my disability. On the one hand, disability sucks; on the other hand, my life is incredible, and I wouldn't trade it for anything. As you read through my reflections, I hope you'll keep one hand for each of those truths.

For friends and readers entering in at year ten of my disability, I need to provide some context of the nearly twenty-five years I had pre-disability (my accident was two and a half weeks before my 25th birthday). I grew up in the suburbs of Portland, Oregon in the Pacific Northwest of the United States, and I was a PDX girl through and through. PDX is the airport code for Portland International Airport and general reference to the city of Portland; PNW is the affectionate local shorthand for the pacific northwest of the United States. I never wanted to leave the PNW, and I expected everyone I ever knew would be familiar with those particular acronyms. When I was in tenth grade, I decided that I wanted my English teacher Mrs. Maki's job when I grew up. I actually stayed on that trajectory for almost nine years. I went to university specifically to get a teaching degree and be licensed to teach English in the state of Oregon. Because I also love learning and the Bible, I ended up at Multnomah University for the majority of my undergraduate degree where I double majored in Biblical Studies and English. I stayed there for my Masters in Teaching as well.

Right out of grad school, God stripped away all my plans to take Mrs. Maki's job. Instead, God shoved me outside my comfort zone to teach me that he had plans for me beyond my wildest dreams. I accepted a job teaching Bible and English at Black Forest Academy in Kandern, Germany, and within weeks of arriving, I knew I'd stay longer than my two year commitment. Two years turned into ten with a significant sabbatical in New Zealand stuck in the middle. I really cherish so much of my Kandern season: the friends I made there, the students I taught, the coworkers who shaped me, the *brötchen*.

A lot of wild and crazy hurt happened during that decade ranging from a broken back to broken trust to a broken dishwasher.

A lot of wild and crazy *healing* happened during that decade as well. My communication skills developed as I practiced writing and sharing my story and even branched out to self-publish a poetry book. My coworker Eric, for whom I already had the utmost respect as an educator and friend, encouraged me to write a textbook for high school students to learn about theology from a more ecumenical and cross-cultural perspective. I found myself regularly included in the "lunch bunch" at my friends' Laurie and Dottie's house as they opened their table to a diverse group of Jesus followers after church many Sundays. My stomach and soul were fed so well at that table. My physio Anja became a friend and one of my biggest champions as I continued to make physical gains post-accident. I've learned so much about holistic health and persistence and grace as she's walked beside me — literally — for the majority of my recovery.

Minus Anja, anything in that paragraph above could have happened without the disability, but hear me clearly, I never want to give up Anja in my life. She's such an incredible friend and encourager. Thinking back to the REHAB days, I've also got Alex and Danai (and Andy and Anna, and Isabelle, and honestly so many more). Even the week before REHAB, I met the university hospital physio Saskia. Saskia was only in my life for the first ten days post-accident, but those were critical. I was terrified and confused, and when I was told the doctors were fighting my insurance to move me to REHAB Basel, I had no idea what that meant. Saskia explained to me, "If I was in your condition, REHAB Basel is the facility I would want to go to." I knew I needed to be there. The way it was explained to me at the time was that I had a 1% chance of learning to walk again and it was only possible if I was at that facility. If I didn't get to do my rehab there, my odds of ever walking immediately dropped to zero.

When I had my accident, I knew very little about disability in general and spinal cord injuries in particular. I trusted experts like Saskia and later Alex and Anja to give me necessary advice and perspective. I've had a steep learning curve with experts and experience to teach me, and while I know a lot more about my own anatomy and physiological triggers, I promise you the biggest learning gains I've had are in the area of patience, perseverance, and my closeness to Jesus. To me, the holistic gains in the area of my emotional and spiritual health are the most valuable. I also promise you that I haven't given up hope on learning to walk (and pee) normally again.

Generally, the audience I've maintained are the people who aren't just here to gawk at my disability. They tend to be people who care about my ongoing physical recovery. Although I'm jumping around a decade span, let's go back to the day I woke up from surgery in the Basel Unispital: I felt severed from my belly-button down, and the only muscle group I had any connection to was my quadriceps. With lots of ups and downs along the way, I have hit significant markers (in no particular order) of: several seconds standing without my braces, hands free, spine stacked and no support; keeping on my feet for over an hour with a standing frame; walking a kilometre independently with just my braces and four-footed crutches; navigating a lap around a physio hall with just hiking poles and Anja's hands on my waist; crossing a small gym with my braces and Mike's encouragement; traveling to over twenty countries on three continents diagnosed as a paraplegic. Significantly, those are not listed chronologically because my recovery has had this "kairos" time where I hit markers of growth but don't necessarily maintain the physical accomplishment ongoing. It's a back and forth battle for recovery. The day I first walked a kilometre, my body needed a lot of rest after. When I hit the half a kilometre daily on the treadmill for a week, I had to stop walking for a month because a massive blister showed up on my foot. Arriving in New Zealand the second time, I didn't have my routines in place for physio, but I still ended up with double blisters on my feet and had to put my attention on other areas of my holistic health during the initial months of my transition.

Five months after I moved back to New Zealand, still within the window experts allow for cultural transition, I worked to establish healthy routines, but did not reach my peak in every area of physical accomplishments. Look back over my brief and far from exhaustive list of physical achievements just listed — they all require different muscle groups, nerve signals, energy levels, and stamina. Taking the ten year look, I'm miles (or kilometres) ahead of my post-op condition — far, far beyond what any medical expert could have predicted. One of the most significant parts of Anja's job of the last decade has been to remind me of the long term perspective. I've come so very far from where I first started. Early on, I often would finish a physio session or personal workout and be disappointed that I couldn't accomplish more, or I'd feel frustrated and angry about the limitations and setbacks a blister brought. Anja gave me the perspective of not only where I had been but the trajectory in which I was heading.

My trajectory includes more physical ability as well as becoming a kinder, more compassionate human being. The most recent years in particular have given me extra opportunities to see how I am a person who needs help physically but that we all need help in some way or another. My limitations and need for help are often linked to physical shortcomings that are direct results of my disability. As I've learned to live relatively well with nerve damage, I've had opportunity to consider and grow in non-disability areas of weakness in messy community alongside other humans made in the image of God. Whatever it means to be made in the image of God, it has to do with relationship; I've grown relationally as I've asked for help, asked for prayer, asked for people to sit with me when I'm feeling low emotionally. Sometimes there's a direct connection to my disability and need for help, but sometimes I'm just human.

I absolutely want to walk again without mobility aids. I crave a miraculous healing today. I dream of full recovery from my nerve damage. But even if that all happened in an instant, I'd still need support. I'd still need community. I'd still need people around me to help me to live to the fullest. I've been publicly posting stories of my life and recovery for a decade, recognising that it's this global village that sees my humanity and prays for me in all these details of my life that allows me to thrive in any physical circumstances. Even able-bodied people need prayer and support from community.

I also want to honour the loose ends and unfinished elements of my story as I pass ten years. I was reflecting with a friend about the tension in writing certain chapters in my memoir because of how I've seen people walk away from Jesus or I have a lack of resolution in my story. I would love to write a reflection here that was a beautiful bow on ten years of tragedy, but if you've been paying attention, that's just fiction. My life isn't a tragedy. It's had a decent amount of trauma, yes, but I'm resilient, and I am in the middle of working through learning from God and figuring out how to live well in any given circumstance. So just past my ten year marker, I want to emphasise that this isn't the end. I'm not at the start, but for the rest of this text, we're hanging out in the middle of my story.

In Medias Res

The tragedy
Welcome to the middle of my story

My life didn't start as a mess filled with grief
My story didn't start with pain and disability
My story didn't start with trauma and heartbreak

Welcome to the middle where I figure things out

Back in the beginning I found true love
Back in the beginning I danced in the rain
Back in the beginning I was full of promise

Welcome to the middle where the promise hasn't left through my tragic plot twist

I'm not sure what the end of the story is, but welcome in medias res. You are here with me in the middle; this isn't the end. I'm writing another chapter, and you're welcome to stay and learn with me the happy ending. I haven't got to that part yet, so I don't know what it is. If you saw me from the start, you would know this won't end a tragedy. It's messy in the middle.

But I'll come out strong
I'll come out beautiful
I'll come out better than before

You can write yourself out of my story
You can miss the final act

I won't judge you for doubting me
I can't promise how this ends
I can only tell you that you met me in medias res

2

On Pain

P ain is a gift.

Pain helps one to know something isn't right in the human body.

Pain is also impossible to perfectly communicate from one person to another. I don't know what your scale of pain is, and you can only guess what I might be feeling. Due to these differences, I don't know what you associate with as something that hurts or inflicts physical agony.

In her famous essay "On Being Ill," Virginia Woolf said the English language didn't have the words to describe pain though she did her best to articulate the isolation brought on by pain and sickness. She said it would take an American to actually describe pain, so I'm here to be bold enough to try. While I can easily come up with rivers of words, I can't articulate the feeling with any universal accuracy. Pain is isolating. This is something you always experience alone — even when you share a tragedy with someone, you experience it from a different perspective.

I felt a lot of physical agony when I broke my back.

I fell ten meters (something like thirty feet for you non-metric folks), and I didn't have time to see my life flash before my eyes before I hit the ground. I just hit the hard floor, and my legs were largely out of commission. Not just for the moment, not just for a while, but for the indefinite future. I was in excruciating torment. It hurt more than I could bear as a tsunami of agony crashed on my brain, and while I didn't want to think about it, pain was overwhelming the nerve signals through my body. Laying on the floor unable to move, I asked the nearest person to tell me a story to distract me. I did not want to think about the physical torment my body was enduring. I was hoping someone would offer me an engaging story to distract me from the crazy loud signals screaming from my spine. A kind German lady knelt by me to ask a steady stream of questions about myself which I only later realised was her gracious attempt to distract me. I did my best to politely answer while hoping I could just listen to someone else talk after each response. I found it difficult to sort through the screaming and confusion in my brain to articulate responses for each question amidst the excessive, relentless pain.

My pain in that moment shattered my previous measurement scale. It was easily a hundred times higher than any pain I'd experienced before.

It hurts when something breaks.

I'm not talking about emotional pain here. We talk about heartbreak a lot, and I think more people have experienced emotional pain than physical, but I think there's something significant in the difference between the two. How can the same word refer to both the thing that rends our souls and the tangible monster that tortures our bodies? Emotional pain is natural — it's part of growing up and maturing. It's not something that disappears as we age, but we come to understand and learn how to deal with it appropriately as healthy adults. "Growing pains" are natural too, so I suppose that is the association that allows us to borrow this word from the physical and apply it to the metaphorical.

I've tried to explain the discomfort I went through in the hospital multiple times. Once I hit the floor, I experienced sharp stabbing pain accompanied by a throbbing sensation materialising in the middle of my waist that would not leave even with loads of morphine in the emergency room. The hours ticked by so slowly before they finally operated. I kept asking if we could just get on with the surgery because I knew I'd be put under anaesthesia which would finally douse the angry flames in my body blazing along my nerves. A fire had been lit by the fracture in my spine, and my brain was overwhelmed trying to explain to me that this was a serious injury.

When I woke up after the surgery, the hospital staff gave me more pain killers. It was a band-aid on a bullet wound situation. I quickly learned the maximum dose they'd give and the minimum number of hours before they'd let me re-up, and I would request the pills at the shortest intervals so that they'd never wear off. The medication masked a lot of torment, but after six hours, I was in agony again. Unfortunately, that meant each night in the hospital I'd wake up from the pain and have to wait the two hours for the drugs to actually kick in again. I spent ten days staring at a dark hospital ceiling with my earbuds in listening to Ryan Clark sing Demon Hunter lyrics louder than my pain. I also thought a lot about Julian of Norwich.

Julian of Norwich knew a lot about the physical sensation of discomfort. She's a Christian mystic from the fourteenth century who once prayed that God would give her a vision of Christ on the cross that allowed her to share in his suffering. I once prayed that God would give me the courage to someday pray that same prayer. To be clear, I never actually made it to that point of asking God for the chance to share in the suffering of the crucifixion. However, I found my chance to share some small measure of agony in the hospital. I taught theology to high school students for a decade, and we talked about the historical details of the crucifixion in my class. Those Romans knew their torture technology. They knew how to rip apart a body and keep it just barely alive for the maximum amount of physical and psychological pain in the prisoner. I was a prisoner on this Swiss hospital bed, and I asked Jesus to teach me what it was like to endure the pain of the cross. Obviously, I was enduring far, far less than Roman torture, but I learned a lot about Jesus who willingly went through even more than a broken back to rescue me from my own sin.

    Pain is an opportunity.

    Pain is a part of the human experience.

    We all experience pain — right?

    Well, apparently, we don't. At least not in the same way.

    The worst part of pain isn't the physical — it's the isolation. Pain can only be experienced within your own body. You can't ever share that experience perfectly. No one can ever really know what level of pain you're enduring. Doctors often ask for a number on a ten point scale, but that's useless if the greatest pain you can imagine is a broken finger and you've never stepped on a Lego barefoot before. My moderate pain may be described as mild by someone else or extreme to a third person. Each scale is relative to our experiences. Anecdotally, I've discovered that I've got some unusually high pain tolerances, but I'm pretty sure a lot of that is related to my overexposure to pain rather than some biological superiority.

    When I was about two, I broke a finger. I don't remember it, but my parents have a great picture of me grinning with a massive cast around my wrist to immobilise the damaged thumb. Family legend has it that I cracked it somehow in a folding chair. Until I broke my back over two decades later, this was the extent of my experience with physical pain from broken bones.

    This is what I've grown to know as true about pain: the more you become familiar with it, the less it hurts.

    That's not necessarily healthy. In fact, I'm pretty sure it's more harmful than healthy. However, recognising it has to be an important first step for me. I've had a lot of physical trauma in my life compared to the ordinary Westerner, and I'm surprisingly at peace with that. I also have a super low patience for people complaining to me that their feet hurt from walking too much. Trade you!

By the grace of God, though, over time, I have developed more empathy towards the pain in others which I can't see. One of the many areas of growth I have experienced in years of chronic back pain is that I complain about my pain a whole lot less to other people. It's got to be a pretty huge deal for me to even acknowledge my pain out loud because for years post accident, I was generally hovering on what pre-accident me would have considered a three or four on the ten-point pain scale. That means headaches, hurt knees, or pulled muscles don't even register until they hit a five — halfway up what my entire concept of pain was previously. I've had to create a whole new pain scale accordingly.

I tried to explain this to my best friend once, and she accidentally flipped the math in her head. She thought that meant that when I felt a level six it would be like when she complained about a level two of pain because I was four points higher all the time.

"You've got to tell me when you're at a six because that's like when I'm telling you about my two level pain, and I want to be able to empathise in the moment."

I didn't have the heart to tell her in the moment that she'd miscalculated. About a year later, it came up in conversation. "It's actually the opposite scale. I'm so used to a four that when a six hits me, it'd be like if you got slammed with a sixteen because I'm so numbed to the first four levels of pain."

Numbed.

I'm numb to what the majority of people would call pain. I'm in that minority of the population that lives with chronic pain or has experienced significant enough physical trauma to have a skewed scale of how much discomfort a pinch might bring.

"Do your legs hurt?" I'm asked all the time.

"Nah, it's just annoying." Just a thousand pins stabbing me every second of contact anywhere below the knee kind of annoying. And a little low buzzing of annoying through my thighs. And some background throbbing in my lower back annoying. But honestly, no one wants to hear those details when they ask about my injury in our first conversation. Sure, I'm in what many would call constant pain, but I've learned to turn up the music of life louder than the pain until it's just the background noise kind of annoying.

"Do you experience pain often?" an exercise physiologist asked me at our first appointment during my week of intensive therapy.

"Well, I kinda always have a dull ache in my lower back, but I just ignore it."

Even now as I type this, I've got my earbuds in, turned all the way up, because I find the distraction from the physical pain a helpful way to focus my attention on the mental tasks before me. (I know the dangers of hearing loss — I've already experienced some of it thanks to loads of Demon Hunter concerts in high school.) I've found my body can be a distraction from so many tasks because of all the physical pain it consistently carries which is why I look hard for ways to cope or compensate for the stiffness and soreness that is my normal.

That's why in the rehab hospital the doctors doubled my pain medication after they discovered I was sleeping it off and trying to cover it with music in the middle of the night instead of being able to rest and recover.

"Pain is the body's signal to the brain that something is wrong," the kind Swiss doctor told me, "We know something is wrong in your body. And the pain is not a helpful message. In fact, right now because all the pain signals are going to your brain, it's preventing you from being able to do anything else. We are going to give you medication to mask the pain so that you can focus on rest and recovery. You'll be able to go off the pain medication eventually, but we don't want you to be distracted by the pain."

I spent the next two months on loads of powerful pain pills. One day I casually asked when I might lower the doses of the pain medication. The next morning I was taken off one of the three types of pain killers. A couple weeks later, we repeated the cycle, and I went down to one pain killer that we reduced at my request over the following weeks. Almost immediately after getting off all the pain killers, my chronic insomnia kicked back in after about a two month hiatus. When the nurses caught on to the fact I was losing sleep, the doctor put me back on oxycodone because he was convinced the insomnia was a symptom of my body being in pain.

I remain unconvinced, and the chronic insomnia was unaffected by medication, so I never refilled that prescription once I left the hospital. The pain is a separate issue. To this day, I cohabit my body with a relatively low level of chronic pain that I don't treat unless it tips past the six on the pain scale I used in the hospital. I'm often hovering around that pre-injury three level of discomfort, but I just negotiate how much attention I give to the pain versus how much I turn the volume up on my music. My life doesn't feel defined by this pain despite the familiarity.

According to the young adult novelist John Green, the problem with pain is that it demands to be felt. I confess, my numbing of the pain is not an erasure, and I've been growing in my awareness of my pain in recent months because I want to live a more holistic life as a human being. A breathing, bodied, broken human being. I'm trying to feel the pain again so that I can acknowledge and release it. I can't share it, so I'm not trying to complain about it, but I'm trying to be more honest with myself about it. When I tell other people it's just annoying, that's okay because they won't be able to participate with me in it anyways. Rather than repressing pain, I'm on a journey of expressing it.

| 19 | — ON PAIN

Physical pain is still a relatively universal experience despite the fact we can never really know how deeply someone feels the pain. When I was the Sunday school coordinator at my church in university, there was a boy in the toddler class who was a biter. I loved this kid, but I dreaded the news each time I heard he'd bitten someone again. It was probably every two or three weeks — so not *every* week, but more frequent than anyone would like. His parents were so embarrassed each time they picked up their son to hear that he'd bitten again.

In the end, the perpetrator's parents had a huge win when the little guy bit his dad at home one day. Dad promptly put the little guy's hand in his grown up mouth and put enough pressure to get a response. The kid never bit anyone in Sunday school again. He finally understood that his actions were inflicting pain on others. Obviously, the dad was not going to put a full force chomp on his kid's hand, but the little one connected the small pain he felt when bitten as something that he did not want to inflict on others in the future.

I think it took me a little longer to learn a similar lesson about inflicting pain on others.

"Give me back my Barbie," I'd tell my sister. If she didn't respond quickly enough, my teeth would clamp onto her wrist until she released my toy.

"*Mooooooom! Laura bit me again!*" she'd scream.

Strong willed child that I was, my parents struggled to get my little brain to realise that I ought to expect pain in response to inflicting it. I somehow always thought I'd get away with it. Inevitably, however, I'd earn myself a spanking, and my mom wanted to make it clear that the pain I felt in my bum was a punishment for my own bad behaviour. If I'd stop biting, I'd stop being spanked.

Well, I just refused to let my mom know that the spankings hurt me at all in the flawed logic that I'd be winning some moral victory. Our family (well, maybe just me, not the whole family) enjoys retelling the story of one particular painful spanking. My mom was sick and tired of the physical punishment not connecting with the psyche of her small child, and she was determined to get a remorseful response from me. She spanked me firmly, and the head of the ancient wooden spoon broke off on contact with my behind.

She cried.

I didn't.

I can confess to you here and now that it certainly hurt. I definitely felt the physical pain, but I stubbornly refused to give my mom the satisfaction of knowing that in the moment. I honestly can't remember the last time I bit my sister or the last time I earned a spanking from my parents. My mom expected me to respond differently to the spanking, and, in fact, my sister did respond differently to the threat of physical punishment. Similarly, my sister never was physically aggressive towards me because she knew she would lose in any physical encounter with me. Were we to have all out wrestled, my stronger muscles and heavier body weight would have pinned her down in seconds beginning in my early grade school years despite the three and a half years age difference in her favour. Her strong aversion to physical pain kept her from provoking me to beat her up. (To be clear, I never physically beat up anyone.)

Though it took me longer to learn than my Sunday school kid, I eventually figured out that inflicting pain on others — including my sister — was not a wise way to live my life. I didn't like the small amounts of pain I had felt in my childhood, and I didn't want to encounter more or increase it among others.

After my spinal cord injury, I learned a great deal more about how to cope with my own physical pain and how others didn't necessarily understand the pain that I was going through. It was humbling to then translate that learning to increase my compassion for the pain that others experience which I cannot see or understand.

Once my bum hit the climbing gym floor, pain has been a constant companion at varying levels of familiarity. The numbness to the physical symptoms that are ever present doesn't mean there aren't flare ups that distract me from the tasks at hand. I've not lost my stubborn streak from childhood, so when I realised that the sensation of pain was going to be with me constantly, I just decided to get on with life.

The doctors wanted to mask the pain with lots of medications to help me to focus on my recovery. Later, when I asked to reduce the dosage until I eventually made my way entirely off them, the pain was always a faint echo at best. Over the years has grown to be something of a friend. Sometimes the pain gives me messages; that's when we're friends. When my legs cramp or ankles pull, it's a sign to check for blisters. Bladder spasms signal my need to catheter. If the pain communicates clearly, I can adjust something in my behaviour to take better care of my body.

Other times, the pain is a bitter nuisance. There are about six possible messages my uncontrollable leg spasms may be trying to communicate, and by far the most frustrating is when they are just bored. The nerve damage makes it difficult for messages to get to my brain from other places in my body below the injury site, and sometimes the signals get ignored until a major problem occurs and brings on even more pain.

Just before the four year anniversary of my accident, I went in for what was now a routine Botox treatment in my bladder to eliminate the spasms that caused discomfort and incontinence. I'd been having strong symptoms (i.e. discomfort and incontinence) for several weeks before my appointment, and I was trying to treat them with over the counter remedies rather than an additional course of antibiotics before the Botox. I'm not a fan of antibiotics.

Let me clarify, I'm a huge fan of antibiotics, but they make me incredibly nauseous.

I avoid taking them whenever possible, and I knew I'd have to take a week's worth of them during the Botox treatment. When I woke up from my procedure, the nurse informed me there was some serious inflammation that needed to be treated with two courses of medications. When I filled the prescriptions, I realised I was on an anti-inflammatory drug for a week followed by a fresh course of antibiotics that would last six weeks.

Six. Freaking. Weeks.

That made for a total of seven weeks solid that I would be on antibiotics.

Seven weeks solid of nausea.

This happened to cover the entirety of my three week Christmas break. On one hand, I was thankful to not be teaching for three weeks of the nausea, but on the other, that meant my five day vacation over New Years was going to be overshadowed by the urge to vomit on the cobblestone streets of Dresden, in the house of theological icon Martin Luther, and on the former site of the Berlin Wall.

My friend Crystal and I had planned the trip weeks before, and I had been looking forward to visiting three new cities in the country I'd called home for the past four years. We were taking the train to each place and had carefully reserved handicapped spots on the transport as well as disabled accessible hotel rooms. It was an incredible trip; Crystal patiently pushed me when my energy was needed to focus on keeping the food in my stomach as I rumbled over cobblestones. We couldn't manage every attraction and museum in our whirlwind trip, and we were also significantly reduced in what we could do because my energy was so quickly sapped by fighting the nausea in addition to the now normal nerve fatigue I face on a daily basis.

– ON PAIN

"I'm so sorry," I told her at dusk on New Year's Eve, "I just don't have it in me to do another museum. I really want to, but I don't have the energy to make it."

"It's fine. I've seen most of them already on my previous visits. We can go back to the hotel."

I think I was asleep by nine. Germans set off large fireworks in the streets and squares in increasing intensity on New Years. People had been lighting off fireworks in the street out our window intermittently, but I was so exhausted it didn't keep me from falling dead asleep. I did wake up when Crystal opened the hotel window just after midnight, and the noise significantly increased as people cheered and lit off more fireworks.

"It's midnight — happy new year!" she told me.

"Happy new year," I mumbled with as much enthusiasm as I could manage.

Mornings are always more difficult for me even when I don't have to deal with nausea and extreme exhaustion because of the leg spasms that routinely increase in the hours when I first get out of bed. I was doing my best to push through the pain with my low energy while Crystal and I made our way to the train station for the first of our long train rides to make it back home. Once we were helped onto the train (European rail stations have a great steel lift for getting me and my wheelchair into the car), I looked for the open seat that we'd reserved for me to transfer into so I could lift my legs onto my wheelchair cushion and massage out some of the cramping that was causing extra spasms.

In my clearly labelled "reserved" seat, there was a stern looking older German man. My German is not great, so Crystal took the lead trying to explain to this man that we'd reserved the seat he was occupying.

"No, I'm disabled," he told us grumpily.

"Yes, but this seat here has a reservation on it. There are other seats available that you can move to," she explained in German.

"No. I'm disabled, and this is the disabled seat. I have medications in this case."

"Can you at least move your case so my friend can stretch her feet into the seat we reserved for me?"

"No. This is my medication. I'm disabled."

The conversation went on for a while, but the man refused to move himself or his suitcase, so both the seats we'd reserved remained occupied, and Crystal ended up sitting on the floor for the next two hours. The pain was evident on my face to Crystal and all the other passengers around us — everyone except the grumpy old man. As soon as we reached the next stop and a couple passengers disembarked, some kind people across the aisle in a non-disabled spot moved to make room for me to stretch my legs while Crystal massaged them; I clenched my fists as I blinked back tears from the pain.

That trip is still a highlight of my first years in Germany because Crystal is an incredible friend, and I refused to let the nausea, spasms, and countless paralysis complications keep me from living an amazing life.

I returned to work with nearly three weeks left on the antibiotics, and I was required to attend some early morning accreditation meetings that first week back in January. Normally, I was excused from teaching the first two periods of the day as well as from many before school meetings because the administration knew that my body takes significantly longer to deal with getting ready in the morning to reduce the leg spasms. I was begrudgingly showing up at these meetings and doing my best just to look like a normal human being rather than one who was fighting the storm raging in my stomach that was battling to keep everything below my esophagus.

Because of a shift in our school schedule, I did have two days a week that I had to come in earlier than I would have liked, but it was only two rather than five days a week. I'd also agreed to teach a student an independent study course, but I'd specifically told my student, Brooks, not to pick A or B period.

"I teach C and F, so you can shuffle your schedule to do independent study with me during D, E, or G period."

I'd written up the curriculum for him to get the special permission to take this class as well as still have a study hall because most independent studies are done during the student's only study hall class. It was one of the few approved independent studies allowing a student to keep an additional study hall period.

"I can only do it during A period, Ms. Hewett, is that okay?" he told me the day before the semester switch.

"Are you serious? You can't do anything else? When is your study hall?"

"It's a conflict with World Views class. I can't move anything else around, and there's not another period that fits in my schedule."

"*Fine*. I'll make it work."

I showed up for A period that first Monday of the semester feeling worse than nearly any other day on the antibiotics. Brooks was eager to learn; we went over the syllabus I'd made up for him and checked out a copy of the textbook he'd be using from the library. I was excited to teach him; he was excited to learn; I hated that it was so early in the morning and my legs were fighting me. Any movement was sloshing around the unsettled food in my stomach.

Despite the second cup of coffee that would normally settle my mood, I was quite irritable when my teacher's assistant arrived during B period. My TA happened to be roommates with Brooks, and I was complaining to my helpful assistant about how I had to come in during A period which meant I'd be at school the first hour of the day four days a week instead of two. My TA accidentally admitted to me that Brooks could shuffle his schedule around but had wanted to keep a study hall with his girlfriend.

As soon as the bell rang, I charged into the hallway to find Brooks and demand he change his schedule around for me. When I'd calmed down a bit the next day, I explained my frustration to him.

"I wouldn't have reacted so strongly if I didn't have another week of this stupid antibiotic. I've been on edge for over a month because of it, but I seriously don't like getting out of bed early to deal with the leg spasms or have to deal with them while at school. I told you to try to do the afternoon periods. You get to spend plenty of time with your girlfriend."

We eventually worked out a system where I did two days a week during A period on the days I was already there to teach beforehand so he could have G period study hall with his girlfriend. I'm not a monster.

Pain is the monster. Pain is the reason mornings are so difficult for me. Pain is the reason I can't get my shoes on easily, can't stand up for long, can't go through my routine too quickly.

Pain is also my friend. Pain is familiar when my body still doesn't make sense to me with the nerve damage. Pain is my companion when I can't explain my isolating experiences. All the respect to Julian of Norwich for inviting the pain of the crucifixion to now Christ better. In my experience, pain has been my invitation for Christ to show me how I am known with compassion and intimacy. Because I can't communicate it perfectly to other humans, I can only cry out to the God-man who has felt the worst physical pain and meets me in my most agonising moments.

3

On Depression

Imagine a big, fuzzy blanket that when draped over you has the effect of sucking the warmth out of you rather than blocking you from the cold. It holds on to you like a blanket of gloom that becomes reassuring after a while because the foggy culprit that has infiltrated your brain makes you think everyone else hates you. It's weighted and dark with sharp but fuzzy edges that can send tendrils into your brain that whisper lies about you and everyone around you. Little needles line the blurry fringe of the dark covering waiting to shred you. It puts a film over your eyes to keep you from seeing the reality of those who love you. It tells you to turn within yourself because you are a burden to others; it fills your inside with self-loathing so that when you do turn within yourself all you see is hate.

That lying blanket of depression is disappointingly familiar to me. The lies that depression most commonly whispers to me are about my identity: You are a burden. You aren't worthwhile. You are a drain on the world. People just put up with you, but you don't contribute anything. You are incapable. You are inadequate. All of these lies came before any experience of paralysis, but some of them were intensified when my spinal cord injury shifted my physical reality. The lies hit me where I am most vulnerable. My deeply rooted insecurities leave me exposed to attacks about my self worth and inherent value as a person.

The lies change depending on the individual. One of my students wrestles with lies related to his existential reality. Another student struggles to reconcile the doctrine she's been taught with the expression of the church in her community which leads to grave doubts about the fundamentals of faith and her reason for living in this confusing world. We all hear lies from the ambiguous "world" out there, but there are some of us who are somehow more susceptible to the whispers in our heads.

Clinical depression affects people differently, and there are loads of studies explaining the various reasons people walk into depression or wade through long periods of melancholy. I can't summarise all those scientific insights, but I can reflect on a strange symptom shared by many people struggling with depression: the lies become a comfort. Like waves crashing relentlessly against the rocks wearing boulders down into sand, people begin to believe the persistent lies over the truth, and, in some cases, even consider extreme options to end the overwhelming voices. In a sermon I heard dealing with this topic, the person preaching explained that suicide isn't a desire for death: it's a desire for life that achieves final peace. Because those whispers won't go away, they become the norm and eventually seem believable when they tell you the world is better off without you.

I'm not a rookie when it comes to depression, and I wasn't before the spinal cord trauma which people expected to launch me into a dark mental health episode. When my accident happened, I'd already weathered through several major depressive episodes in my past where I seriously considered ending my life, and I've had multiple subsequent to the accident — though, significantly, not one in the hospital or during the immediate period after my accident.

– ON DEPRESSION

A week after finishing my third grade year, I had my last playdate with Jessica. I was sobbing and waving goodbye out the backseat of my mom's minivan as we pulled away from her house for the last time. I didn't know if I'd see her ever again as Jessica's family was moving to Minnesota that week. After I spent the summer crying over the loss, I found myself alone with thoughts of ending my life. As a chubby, insecure fourth grader, I struggled to find friendships as close as the one I lost the year before. It wasn't that I thought that Jessica was my only friend or only reason worth living, but that separation was the catalyst that set my delicate brain off. My mom was struggling through her own depression, and I think I subconsciously picked up on the fact that life was stressful for her as she coped with this mental sickness while raising two kids and maintaining a healthy marriage.

I tried not to be a bother, but I ended up being an overweight, anxious little kid, worried about triggering my overwhelmed mom; the depression blanket wrapped around me whispered in my ears that I was significantly more work to care for than my seemingly perfect sister.

"You'd be helping your family if you just left. You can't run away because they would have to look for you. You need to be dead so that you won't worry them anymore." After several weeks, the voice was pretty convincing. The lies were much more prevalent in my head than the vocalisation of the truth despite the fact that I had two loving parents and a considerably stable home life. I remember listening to this dark inner narrative while I stood in my bedroom and stared at the string on the mini-blinds. Could I tie that around my neck and jump off the bed to hang myself? I pulled the string. What a stupid idea, I realised almost instantly. It would only get tangled up and yank the whole contraption off the window, creating a greater problem as I'd have to explain why I was tied up in the mini-blinds when my parents found me completely alive with a ruined window covering. I felt foolish for considering the voice.

It didn't give up though. Not too long after, I found myself standing in the kitchen staring at the butcher block and hearing the voice tell me, "You won't survive if you just keep stabbing yourself. By the time someone finds you, you'll be dead for sure. It won't fail. You just have to get the resolve to help your family by ending your life. You're just being selfish taking up all their attention and adding to the stress in their life. You should just stop being so selfish and stab yourself. End this now."

I listened. I stepped forwards and reached out my hand for the largest knife. Before I reached it, I felt an unseen hand hold my little arm back. I couldn't move myself forward anymore. In my head, I saw clearly the image from the Sunday school story of Abraham offering Isaac when the angel holds back Abraham's hand. My fourth grade brain was convinced an angel was there holding my hand back because I wasn't supposed to kill myself.

Just as the descent into that difficult season was a spiralling process, the climb back to normal mental health also took time. While it was difficult to see in the moment, I know a lot of my journey out of depression was thanks to the supportive mom who recognised what I couldn't understand myself.

When I finally began counselling in high school, I learned a lot of really helpful tools to be able to deal with the lies that the depression would whisper to me. It would wrap me up and tell me that my friends didn't want me to be around and that I was never going to be good enough for them. It sucked all the warmth out of my friendships and told me I was all alone which only made me pull the dark blanket closer. I felt so cold, so exposed, so lonely, but the depression could wrap around me to keep me covered with the imitation of being close to something. The foggy tendrils of depression kept me from realising that the closer I pulled the blanket to fight the cold, the more it sucked the warmth out of me.

ON DEPRESSION

Scientists, parents, and youth leaders like to brag that high school brains aren't fully developed, but that doesn't diminish the emotions that rage inside the minds of teenagers. I was no exception when I was sixteen. After my social world fell apart, I found myself drowning in a pretty severe bout of depression.

I can remember reading the email that my best friend sent me telling me that I was a horrible human and the world would be better off without me. That was the subtext. And some of the text came pretty close. It wasn't a long email, but it got to the point that I ought to be ashamed of my behaviour and do everyone a favour by killing myself. At least, that was the effect that came across.

I first read it on a Sunday morning. I hadn't seen that friend on Saturday. I don't remember what happened on Friday. I just remember the stunned feeling I had as I fumbled to the car and drove myself to church. Highway 26 never had much traffic on Sunday mornings, and when I was a high school student, we lived far enough out in undeveloped Hillsboro that there was a long stretch of road in front of me and grass on either side of me while I contemplated the words I'd just read.

"Just pull the wheel to the left. Crash the car. If your *best friend* thinks you should be dead, there is definitely no one else who wants you alive. You're just a burden on your family. End this all right now."

I heard the thoughts in my head as though they were whispered by someone else. Like the images in movies of the devil on my shoulder giving me the idea as an entity separate from myself.

Just as separate from my own mind came the response: "You wouldn't actually kill yourself. There's nothing to crash into; you'd just wreck the car and wrack up huge hospital bills. Then your parents really will hate you even more than they already do."

Calling that the voice of an angel isn't quite right though I'm comfortable describing the whole situation as some form of what Christians call spiritual warfare. Similar to the fourth grade experience, something in my brain connected the fact that I wouldn't guarantee my own death with this plan. Instead, all I could guarantee was huge medical bills and upped insurance payments for my parents. Something in my brain was offering logic as a literal life preserver in the ocean of emotion in which I was drowning.

I managed to keep my car on the road and pull into the church parking lot. Taking a few deep breaths, I entered the church, taught my lesson, and found my youth leader between services.

"I just thought about killing myself on the way to church. It's been a rough week. Can you pray for me?"

"Oh my gosh, another girl just told me she tried to kill herself too this week. It's been a rough week for our small group."

I know the words were meant to somehow console me — probably. However, I heard them as a one-up on my bad morning. I excused myself and spent the rest of the church service wondering why I was in that small group when the leader didn't seem to care about my issues. It's not surprising that the voice I'd just battled on the drive to church spent the next several hours trying to tell me that I really ought to commit suicide so that the youth leader could focus her attention on keeping the student that actually mattered alive.

I don't remember the drive home; my brain blacked out until I made it home on auto-pilot knowing I needed help if I was going to keep myself alive. As soon as I walked into the house, I found my mom standing in the kitchen.

"I need counselling," I collapsed on the floor in tears after my confession. She immediately crossed to where I was and held me.

"I'll call the pastor tomorrow to find a list of counsellors."

"Can we afford that?"

"That's not even an issue, Laura."

She immediately sprang into action, and I was in a counsellor's office with her in less than three days. My mom came with me to the first appointment, and since she had made all the calls, she knew which office to go to when we arrived at the bland corporate building in downtown Beaverton.

A short, round woman with glasses and a soft smile welcomed us into her office with significantly cheerier colours than the waiting room. I took a seat on the overstuffed loveseat next to my mom. I was wearing my puffy white coat, too uncomfortable to take it off despite the warm room. Dr. Lennert settled into a matching comfy chair next to the loveseat. I was perched on the edge, ready to bolt, but something about her sitting comfortably put me somewhat at ease. I talked to Dr. Lennert with my mom there for a bit, then my mom stepped out into the waiting room, and I answered a few more questions without the parental supervision.

When my mom stepped out of the room for the second half of the session, I explained the email that triggered my fateful drive.

"I know it's dumb to let an email make me think that I should die, but it was from my best friend. I don't know what I did to make him so upset with me. I don't know how to just ignore it and move on. I'm really scared to be around people because I don't want to upset them. I've been avoiding people as much as I can at school."

"What have you been eating?"

"Oh, um, well, I don't really like lots of meat and heavy food, and I'm allergic to nuts, so I don't eat those. And I haven't really been interested in fruits or veggies lately, and breads make me feel kinda sick these days. Um, actually, I haven't really been eating much of anything the last few days. Except for peppermint tea. That makes me feel calm."

Dr. Lennert was professional in her assessment, casually noting down the symptoms I had and my own lack of awareness to my situation.

I wore my puffy winter coat to therapy each week. I sat in the same spot on the loveseat in the office, perched on the edge, never completely settling in. Dr. Lennert kindly wrote down notes occasionally and asked polite questions to nudge me along in my processing and narratives. Just over six months past my first session with Dr. Lennert, I drove myself through the afternoon traffic to the now familiar business parking lot, walked up the drab staircase, entered the bland reception area, and waited to be invited into the cheery office.

I was still wearing the puffy white jacket at the end of the six months; I wore it every week. I wore it every day. It zipped up tight around my torso and hugged me into my insecurities. I never let my body be physically comfortable in most spaces, and I realised it that last week as we ended the session. Now that I finally felt safe enough to settle into the space, I was healthy enough to not need to come back to it.

"I think you've found hope," Dr. Lennert was telling me, "I don't think you need to come back for regular sessions. You've learned a lot of skills through the past few months, don't you think?"

"Yeah," I had half my attention on the conversation that we were finishing. I knew that I didn't need to come back, but I looked around at the little table with building blocks and colouring papers. I noticed the six other places I could have made myself comfortable to sit in the carefully arranged furniture. I realised for the first time how soft the loveseat actually was and how comfortable it would be to settle back and take my coat off.

"Yeah," I repeated with a little more confidence, "I think I'll be okay... I know I will."

"Yes, and you can always call me and set up an appointment in the future if you find that you need to talk again."

She handed me her business card as I walked out.

"Thank you," I smiled.

It was a real, genuine, heartfelt smile. I'd found hope, and I was going to be okay. I didn't want to kill myself, and I was going to survive high school.

I tucked her business card into my wallet and kept it there for the next seven years. It moved along with all my credit cards, coffee punch cards, and insurance cards to every new wallet up until my move to Germany. It was a comfort to see it as I pulled out cash at the mall or paid for my Starbucks. I knew I could always call Dr. Lennert if I needed to, and that assurance helped me never need to.

Dr. Lennert didn't need to rush me through the process of finding hope, but I wanted to make progress and get away from depression. She never shamed me when I recounted what I considered to be embarrassing social interactions — looking back, it's certainly because they were just the kind of high school dramas that only felt huge in the moment because I was still dealing with the wispy lies curling in and out of my mind from the depression. Though it felt like a significant portion of my life in the moment, time in her office was just a blip in my junior year of high school.

What I remember most of that year is the darkness. The loneliness. The self-loathing. I can still readily recall those emotions — because they haunt me still. I learned critical tools from Dr. Lennert on how to battle those emotions effectively — how to speak truth to the lies when they manage to settle in. Perhaps the most important thing I learned from my time in counselling was that there was no shame in being someone who deals with depression. I also know from the statistics that it's increasingly likely to return to someone who's had it before. My brain is somehow prone to these misfirings, and I need to have my skills sharp to fight against it. Each time depression settles in, I learn something new about how to handle the physical, emotional, mental, and spiritual attacks of depression.

As a sixteen year old, I didn't know that what people thought of me wasn't as important as what God thought of me. Sure, as a church kid I knew the concept intellectually, but I'd built up a persona that was intertwined with my best friend being super popular and validating me as a person. When he told me I was a worthless person and tossed me aside, I watched what felt like the whole school turn against me as he made our whole social group choose sides between us. Ultimately, I discovered there was an entire subculture of students in my tiny school that didn't like this popular kid, and they welcomed me in with open arms when I was an outcast of the upper social stratosphere.

In the subsequent rounds of depression, there remains a scar from the lie that I'm disposable as a friend. Depression tries to tear into the old wound and infect me, but one of the tools I've learned since is that my scar has been redeemed. That skin is thicker than before. I don't have to believe any lie that I'm a worthless person because I've learned from Jesus that I'm worthwhile to him.

I didn't have eloquent language or effective metaphors when I previously tried to explain depression to my eternally peppy college roommate, and I could see the confusion on her face when I tried. What I did realise through my own years of youth ministry work, though, was that I could emote directly with some of my students who dealt with the same heavy darkness. Nothing substitutes for experience.

I saw it on Alyssa during her last year of high school. It sucked away her appetite, and she would rarely eat; I remembered my nearly two weeks of living off peppermint tea because all other food made me nauseous when I looked at it while the depression told me I wasn't worth feeding. My door was always open to Alyssa that year, and I'd make her a cup of tea and open my cupboards to let her eat anything she didn't think she'd throw up immediately. I took to keeping ice cream in my freezer just for Alyssa because there was a chance she'd eat something if I had the right flavour. We'd sit in my living room and talk about her day, talk about the weather, and talk about the nature of the soul. When the days were short, our talks were long, and as spring came, some green leafy bits of hope pushed through Alyssa's heart. I've been privileged to watch these blossom despite stormy life circumstances. Her road hasn't been easy, but she chose to take the offered hands to lead her out of the depression and into the light when she was in high school. She remains one of my closest friends and favourite humans on the planet. Like most people who've experienced depression, it is something that has recurred in her life. Rather than giving up, Alyssa battles with courage and resilience, looking for ways to return to health each time depression tries to knock her down. She will not describe herself with the confidence I assign her, and I want to honour the struggles she still walks through as she seeks to live her life with honesty and integrity.

By the time Alyssa first showed up at my house in high school telling me she couldn't eat and wasn't sure what had happened during her day because everything went by her in a grey blur, I had slightly better language to explain to her mom why she wasn't able to eat anything at dinner with her family or engage as fully in lively conversations. I acknowledge that my blanket metaphor is imperfect to describe depression to someone who hasn't ever experienced it, but I can empathise with those covered in the blanket and attempt to reassure their loved ones that it doesn't have to be a permanent change. I can't, however, make the significant step of casting off depression for anyone else.

A couple of years after Alyssa graduated, I walked alongside another student who had the depression blanket settled on his shoulders as a mantle. Different to Alyssa, he wore it with pride. I watched him shove people away as he pulled the blanket tighter around himself. He looked for ways to cover himself with the depression to hide himself from those who wanted to share any love with him. I don't have the words to explain to him that this is hurting him; I don't need to — he already knows it.

And yet, depression is the closest friend to him. It's familiar at this point. It gets that way.

Unlike Alyssa, this student graduated still guarding his darkness. He chose to reject the offers of help from loved ones and refused to follow through with counselling or medication. In one conversation with me after graduation, he confessed a new belief that the sad version of himself was the real one and that he had no desire to be happy again because happiness didn't feel like the real version of him anymore. I couldn't convince him that was a lie.

When I was suicidal, I still believed that life is precious; I just wasn't convinced that my own was to be included in that. Depression can mess with your logic like that. I've got enough safety nets in place now that when that particular logical fallacy creeps back into my head, I'll be safe enough to shut it down. I do remember being convinced that I'd never manage to be happy again though — that my default existence was in the darkness. That was round three of depression for me. I'd spent time convinced that I'd never be able to cast out the darkness that settled into my mind, tangling lies with my thoughts and confusing me about my identity and worth as a human. Round four looked similar though I fought back with more strength.

Round five of major depression in my life was vastly different than any previous iteration. I saw it coming. I waved as it approached. And I spent fifteen months wrapped up in the coldness telling me that I was an inconvenience to people who I considered friends. I heard it echo the lies that people in my Kandern community considered me a burden because I begged for rides and walks and needed more help than most people. Truthfully, I don't need that much extra help, and the people who've volunteered to take time to drive me places or go for walks with me actually find me to be an enjoyable person to spend time with. However, I still listened to the dark whispers that said I was asking for too much, that I was a slacker for still needing so many people to assist me. Plus the weight of the blanket made each step I took heavier.

When I was a kid, the heavy steps didn't matter. I was the chubby kid in class, the last one in every race in PE, but I knew that wasn't the end of the world because I could still finish. Now, post paralysis, the depression sapped all my energy and then poured shame on me for doing so little physically. People had paid for me to go to physical therapy, and I couldn't force myself to walk the three hundred meters to and from school anymore. I was regressing physically because the depression kept me from walking on my own, and the people who'd given their time to walk with me were not able to see positive results from their efforts either. I was only wasting their time when I asked for help. I needed to be doing it on my own, and I should have accomplished more.

In that round of depression, I knew that I was a worthwhile human and didn't feel at all at risk of suicide, but I did still have to actively fight against the whispers that I was a lot of work to be around or be friends with. I had built up several friendships during my few years in Germany, but all of them were thrown into doubt during this round.

Did these people who claimed to be my family in Christ actually want to love and accept me fully or did they only want me if I was going to be able to offer them something useful in return for their friendship?

I had heard echos and rumours that people were worried I was going to be a burden on the missionary community in Kandern if I chose to stay in town after my accident. No one dared to say that to my face — it just took a couple people to imply that I need to be cautious in asking for help. To be clear, this was a minority. The vast majority of the community around me reached out and offered me help — more than I needed. There was even one coworker who encouraged me to take the help I didn't need because it gave others the opportunity to be connected to me as family in Christ. I was completely humbled by the outpouring of love while still haunted by the stigma of being so needy. I found a comfortable pattern of asking for the help I needed without shame by year four, but then I saw my old friend depression coming down the road. I settled in for what I knew would be another tough battle. I didn't realise this one would be so long, and I didn't realise that I would still struggle with the same insecurities of my worth.

During that round of depression, I was mentoring kids and teaching theology, and dozens of teenagers sought me out to talk to me about deep questions related to what we believe and how we live it out. I was delighted to foster those conversations; I was eager to point them towards Jesus. I was anchored to my Saviour and able to be used by him to love on these kids even while depression crouched in the corner ready to pounce on me the moment the students walked out of my kitchen with their freshly baked cookies.

Was I really making a difference in students' lives? Did it matter that I showed up for work each day when my coworkers didn't like me? Were they just putting on a show out of pity or for the free food? Who else didn't really want me around?

All the while, people were inviting me to dinner, including me in social plans, reaching out to me to encourage me in my walking. The most difficult lie to fight was that the invitations were genuine. I spent over a year feeling like people would only ask me to do anything out of pity for me. Significant to my journey out of depression, the majority of these people kept asking even when I initially declined. They didn't let me wallow in my own darkness and were influential in gently guiding me out.

Near the end of the depression, I asked my friend Cindy to go for a walk with me. I'd refrained from asking her often because of the fear that she would only say yes out of obligation and potentially come to resent ever offering to spend her valuable time helping me. We managed what was to me a huge accomplishment at the time — walking from my house to the bench along the river with no braces. We sat down at the bench for me to recover some energy before closing the loop back to my house. During the rest, I confessed to Cindy that I'd spent a long time refraining from asking often because I'd been fighting the lies that I was a burden to her. She lovingly told me that I was actually offering her an opportunity to spend time with a friend and that it was an added bonus that she was able to use some of her physical therapy training.

When I listened to the lies creeping in from the depression, I was actually depriving people of a friendship with me. I'm worth being friends with. My whole paradigm shifted in that moment as I realised the depression wasn't just affecting me. It was affecting those around me.

I thought back to watching my mom go through depression when I was a kid. She was in so much turmoil, and she did her very best to hide it from my sister and me. I didn't understand everything, but I knew she was hurting, and I wanted to make her feel better. It wasn't her fault, and I'm so proud of her for working hard every day to still be the best mom around while figuring out how to battle through her mental health struggles. I think often about my students who deal with the same problem. I've seen some come out of the dark cloud as champions who know how to face the lies in the future with grace and strength from God. I see others who are so tangled up in the cold lies of depression that they have forgotten what it's like to be in the warm sun with friends. I ache for those children who are too covered in lies to understand they are closed off from the truth.

My experience with depression doesn't give me immunity from sadness or loneliness, but it does give me exponentially more empathy for those who are dealing with the same things. My prayer is that bearing witness to this darkness, this heaviness, can offer insight to others to have compassion towards the friends who default to retreating inside a cold blanket when they ought to go for a walk with you. Don't forget about them, and keep asking to include them in your life.

4

On Dying

"I'm a breath; I'm a vapour," the Skillet lyrics read like a line of Ecclesiastes. The Preacher, the title of the author of the biblical text of Ecclesiastes, instructs readers that all life is a vapour, though some translations say "meaningless." I've listened to some great theologians talk about how that's not the best translation of the connotation because it's about the passing nature of the life we have. The King James Version and the English Standard Version translate the word as "vanity," which still falls short of the idea of brevity rather than our modern connotation of vanity as self-centredness. The Christian Bible gives a lot of space to the fleeting material world and emphasises our eternal nature. It's a tension a lot of Christian artists, authors, and musicians spend a lot of time unpacking.

One of my "go to" songs reflecting on this temporary tension of our eternal soul in mortal bodies is the Skillet song "Vapor" from the album *Alien Youth*. I've been a fan of the band Skillet since I was six. I think of that song whenever I read Ecclesiastes or when I think about death. It's a happy song, as far as songs about our mortality go with lines like, "And the future's robbing my soul, inhaling my mortality." I don't feel sad when I listen to the rock melody. I also don't feel all that sad when

I think about my own mortality or impending death, so maybe it's a me thing more than the catchy beat.

I'm aware that Christians are conflicted theologically on this tension between our mortal and eternal lives and where to focus attention in the already-but-not-yet kingdom.

On the one hand, Christians are supposed to recognise that, just like Jesus, we will conquer death in our future victorious resurrection where we can reign eternal with our Saviour King. It's a great vision of eternity, so why would we be upset about the temporary death of our fading, fallen bodies? The Apostle Paul tells us that we get a resurrected body "raised immortal." It's an upgrade. Personally, I'm looking forward to my 2.0 body that doesn't have the same leg spasms and bladder issues that I currently have to deal with. When my friend Joyce passed away several years ago, all my friends familiar with her long journey with disability commented how she's now dancing with Jesus now, no longer confined by her physically limited body. I want a similar celebration at my own death.

On the other hand, theologically, Death is an enemy to be destroyed. Sure, we have the promise of an ultimate victory, but it's still a bad guy. It's not really a friend, despite the Harry Potter story of the Deathly Hallows that makes Death seem like a chill dude if you trick him into cutting you a slice of his invisibility cloak. Death is the child of sin, the monster that consumes and is never satisfied. Jesus had to conquer death because it was devouring humanity, running rampant in the wake of our sinful choices. So, that's not great, and it's a decay of my body that makes death an inevitability. Scientists have yet to find a cure for death because, well, Jesus is the only one.

Just a couple songs after "Vapor" on that fabulous Skillet album is the song "You Are My Hope." I used that song in my major paper on the word "hope" during my first year of high school. I went back and read the analysis to see if I said anything insightful I could share in this chapter; I didn't. But I do think it's significant that the song has stuck with me. I have much more insightful things to say about it now that I've lived some more life and understand some more about hope in connection with my mortality and promise of eternity. The second verse of the song begins, "Far beyond what I can see or comprehend, etching your eternity in me." I don't have an experience of eternity because I was born in a temporal existence. However, the promise of eternity is etched on my soul, and it's a nice esoteric vision provided in Christianity (and, to be fair, many religions).

Death is real, and I'm going to die someday. That's supposed to make me sad, but I can't help but think of death as a sweet release from my current disabled body. The Apostle Paul talked about how excited he was about being in the presence of the Lord when he died, but he also said to live is a beautiful gift because he gets to do more work for the Lord. I'm pretty much in agreement with his sentiment.

I don't want to hurry it along, I guess. I think that's because as insecure as I am, I know that I've got work left to do here, so I'll keep working to the best of my ability. I learned that lesson from my grandpa when he was dying.

When I was a little kid, I thought he was the funniest person in the world. He always made me laugh. He died of a rare blood cancer, but he lingered on for a long time. In the final months, he was going into the cancer ward to get blood transfusions several times a week. He made all the nurses and other patients laugh. He brought joy and laughter everywhere he went.

"That's my ministry now: keep 'em laughing in the cancer ward." He told me that with absolute conviction, and I remember being awed by his dedication to always find a ministry opportunity even when he was dying. His particular diagnosis wasn't one of those gentle cancers. It was painful and drawn out. He was an old dude, and he'd lived lots of good life up until then, but he wasn't getting a first class pass through the end of life. He slept a lot in his last weeks, and I remember walking through the pale, beige hallways of the retirement home to his room and finding him sleeping fitfully on a big bed. Although we tried to be quiet, the family members shuffling in would wake him up, and then tears would fill his eyes.

"I just want to go home," he'd cry. Every night for those last weeks of his life, he went to sleep hoping that he'd wake up in heaven. Every night that he went to sleep, I hoped that he'd wake up here on earth and make me laugh again. His conversations were less and less coherent as his mind was exhausted from the physical toll the disease was taking on his body. My oldest uncle lived close enough to visit every day, and at the funeral, Uncle Vance told me that he was pretty sure the last fully lucid conversation that Grandpa Frank ever had was with me on my last visit.

I cried when Grandpa Frank died. I cried when Uncle Vance died several years later. In the moment, those were both emotionally heavy experiences for me. And yet, those two funerals are celebrations in my mind. Both of those men were deeply committed to Jesus and lived their whole lives creating a legacy of loving God and loving others well. Hearing the stories of other people who were inspired to live more generously because of those men is incredible. When my grandpa was a young man, he applied to Missionary Aviation Fellowship with his friend Nate Saint. Nate was accepted and martyred shortly after while my grandpa was rejected by the mission agency. My grandpa instead spent his life sharing Jesus as an Air Force pilot in the Philippines, a vastly different story than Nate's. Uncle Vance was involved with founding and funding mission work that is still carried on in Peru. Their legacies after death honour the lives they lived, and there's something quite beautiful about that.

Death is a brutal enemy. I still mourn that these men are not sharing the love of Jesus with people on earth today. Again, as a Christian, I'll still be confident in the ultimate defeat of death that will let me one day see Grandpa Frank and Uncle Vance in resurrected bodies better than their frail and decaying ones I last saw them in.

I'll get a better body too, and, selfishly, I'm totally into that idea.

I do frequently get asked by students if I think that we will have our scars on our bodies when we are resurrected. Jesus still has his scars in the post-resurrection narratives, but there are theologians who have written about this being necessary. I've got no fancy pants Bible proof for this, but I want some of my scars to stay, so I'm going to ask for them.

I spent hours thinking about this after I read the Eragon series while I was in the hospital. There's a beautiful story arc where the protagonist is badly wounded and has this massive scar across his back. It even has limiting effect on his fighting, and he has to learn to adjust to live and thrive with the disability. As a newly disabled person, I was loving the narrative. Then out of nowhere, there's a magic cure for the kid. Like, legitimately it was magic because it's a fantasy novel with elves who can do convenient things like make your scars freaking disappear. I was crushed. Why couldn't they heal the disability and leave the mark as a permanent reminder?

I want my wounds to be redeemed when I'm resurrected. Well, actually, I want them to be redeemed now, but after death, I want to remember the good the Lord has done in my body. My scar on my back is long and thin where the metal was put in to stabilise my spine, and there's a shorter, slightly fatter one over my left hip where the surgeon went to take some bone marrow to strengthen the titanium she screwed into my spine. They tell an important part of my story, and I don't want it to be erased in my new body.

Don't get me wrong, I want to get up and dance in that new body, but I want to have the marks of who I was shaped to be during my life on earth.

Scripture tells us that Jesus still has scars on his hands and feet, and he's a different case than all the rest of humanity, so I recognise that it's not proof I'll keep mine, but I think he'd agree to let me because they testify to the healing work he's done in me. Death can't erase the scars that have been redeemed.

Ultimately, I don't think I'll care that much about the scars when I get to spend eternity with Jesus, but right now, my body is significant to me.

Each of us cares about our body, despite having lots of personalised fights with it as well. When I look in the mirror, I see the ageing body that will one day die, but that's not usually my first thought when I see myself. Usually it's more like, "Can anyone else notice that dead tooth looks a shade darker today than yesterday?" or "Why can't the short hair stay tucked behind my ears?" I don't spend loads of time musing on my imminent mortality. I know other people do. I have lots of conversations with students who are pondering the implications of the eternal in light of their mortal decay. I also have other conversations about the most effective way to ask a girl to banquet. The juxtaposition of life and death is relevant to us all.

The penultimate song on the *Alien Youth* album is called "Will You Be There?" and it's a series of questions about whether God will be near when we approach death or any other struggle. It's all the same. I need God to be near me when I approach death, but I also need him when I struggle through life.

Grief is a normal thing in the face of death, and I won't run away from it, but I won't let it consume me either. Nor will I let fear of death take up any space in my life. It's an unavoidable truth, but I can still celebrate the life I have now and the life to come. I can fight to be an advocate for life in the face of attacks from any source without fear of losing my own temporary physical existence. Christians are supposed to be unafraid of death, and while most of us still have the very human natural fear, mine seems to run a bit lower.

I made a bet with a super competitive student that he would die before I did. Joke's on him because I win either way: I actually plan to die first and lose the stated bet, but he will wait to die until I've died first, so I win. It made a lot of sense in context, and I have asked him to give the eulogy at my funeral. This particular student was experimenting with nihilism in high school — death is no different than life and all that crap. He's actually a super brilliant kid, and we've had lots of existential conversations post high school. I can make jokes with him about my death because he knows that I firmly believe that life is precious.

The conversations about death and the value of life are still shockingly heated within the Christian school context I worked in. Among my peers on staff, there are a wide variety of opinions and passions about the death penalty and various approaches to gun control — defending life on all sides of every issue.

When we added a half hour "Access" period to our school schedule, my classroom inadvertently became the default location for students to pick up these kinds of topics and discuss them. I'd advertised it as a place to talk about theology and continue the class discussions in the extra time, but there were a handful of students who consistently showed up to talk about how their theology impacted their political views and other very practical outcomes in their lives of what they claimed to believe.

I shouldn't have been surprised when the three most politically passionate students trooped into my room seconds after the bell rang to end class and begin the Access period on February 15, 2018. The Parkland shooting had just happened the day before in America, and it had made headlines as the deadliest high school shooting in the country.

"Okay, let's talk about gun control," the Democrat told the Republican as the two sat down on opposing sides of a row of desks.

The Democrat had his politically aligned best friend next to him, and the three students launched into a highly nuanced, very intense thirty minute debate that was occasionally interrupted by Julia passing around Ritz crackers. She was sitting next to the Republican for moral support, but she's generally not interested in politics as much as her friends are. Julia is highly capable of adding to any conversation she's interested in, and later in the school year she initiated a formal debate with one of her male friends about the value of the term "feminism" and how it was important that he support the cause. The boys didn't realise it that day when they were talking about guns, but she kept the humanity in the room when they delved deep into their policy theories.

"Guns don't make places safer," the Democrat began.

"They do if the person is well trained. I feel safer knowing my grandma has her gun wherever she goes because she knows how to use it," the Republican responded.

"But it would be a terrible idea to start arming teachers because they don't all have the training. No one wants Ms. Hewett to have a gun."

"I don't want her to have a gun if she's not trained, but if she or another teacher was trained and willing, I would feel safe with them being armed."

"I don't want a gun," I added, not really wanting to be in the conversation but feeling strongly about that particular point.

"Do you want a cracker?" Julia asked.

"Yes, thank you."

"Okay, but if we armed the teachers who were willing to be trained, we make it easier for them to become the school shooter. It isn't always a student who is the criminal. It's just adding more guns in places that should be gun free." My Democrat student was less interested in snacks than I was.

Aside from the cracker breaks, they went non-stop until the bell rang to end the school day. I listened carefully, interjecting as little as possible except when I was used as an example. No one wants me to have a gun, and there's no room for ambiguity on that one. When the bell did ring at the end of the period, I asked them, "Do you each want to know what you've got wrong in your argument?"

"Yes," they both told me immediately.

"You," I turned to the Democrat, "are forgetting that you're talking about people made in the image of God. When you list off statistics about how many lives would be saved, you forget about the freedoms you're infringing upon of individuals who are just as valuable as the statistics. And you," I continued facing the Republican, "You are forgetting that you're talking about people made in the image of God. When you talk about wanting 'good guys' to take out the 'bad guys,' you are dismissing the fact that the 'bad guys' are just as human as everyone else. They are capable of being victims in their own way."

"Ms. Hewett, we were talking about politics not theology."

They made the mistake of trying to do that in my classroom. Everything is about theology. In their defence, those particular students often built passion around political issues because they saw such a strong connection between what they believe and how they choose to vote. However, what frustrated me was that despite all the other nuance they brought into the conversation, none of my students were talking about real people living or dying in their hypothetical school scenarios.

It's so easy to dehumanise other people when we think about the atrocities someone commits. I'm not perfect when it comes to this. I struggle to speak about certain people who are in charge of policies that lead to the death of hundreds or thousands as fully human because their actions seem so inhumane. I try to read headlines through the lens of my theology as I purposefully consider everyone made in the image of God — victims and perpetrators alike.

It's a theological issue for me here. Even those bringing death are still made in the image of God.

I was in Christchurch, New Zealand, the day of the mosque shootings, and apart from the day of the incident, the shooter's name has been carefully kept from the news coverage. There was even one printed display at the public memorial that had a condemnation of the violence which originally named the shooter but when I visited, another mourner had carefully ripped the name from the page to leave the condemnation of hate without glorifying the name of the shooter. I often used to pray for the broken young man who was bent so far into darkness that he chose to violently slaughter other humans while they were praying. Within about half an hour, fifty people were killed and fifty more were wounded by a single person. Every life in that count matters, and according to my theology, the terrorist also retains his humanity despite his unrepentant heart.

Fortunately, I also believe in a just God who can make sense of a world filled with the brokenness of death and sin.

Christians spend lots of time talking about the doctrine of original sin and how we all have inherited sin nature but we are only liable for our own sins. When I teach my students about sin nature, we talk about how it's something that all people have to deal with, and we all have the option of Jesus saving us from the punishment of sin. Then we talk about the verse in the book of Romans that teaches "the wages of sin are death."

I'm a victim of death, whenever I die. I'm also a perpetrator of sin. Death is the child I've conceived since the book of James says that sin gives birth to death. I'm getting into the esoteric elements of theology, but it changes the way I live.

If I know death is inevitable based on my sin, I could choose to throw up my hands and give in now, but I love the beautiful life I get to lead where I get to teach teenagers about theology.

Bear with me for this tangent because I promise it will connect in a minute.

A couple years ago there was a big controversy surrounding the book made into movie which was about a wheelchair bound guy and one of those ordinary filler girl characters. I won't read or watch them on principle. I had a really great conversation with my sister about how conflicted I was that an able bodied woman would write a book about how life in a wheelchair was so depressing that it just wasn't worth living anymore. That's the message that came across to the majority of the disability community in the reviews that I read. I refuse to give any money or attention to a message like that. My life may suck sometimes, but it sucked sometimes when I could walk too. Don't tell me I'm better off dead because of the spinal cord injury. Think very carefully before you drop the phrase, "I'd rather die than live like you," especially in front of someone with a disability.

If I had died instead of moving to the wheelchair, I would never have taught the bright spot in humanity that is Julia. My death is inevitable, but that particular gem gives me a tiny bit of immortality as I know she has learned something from me that carries on in her life whenever I do die just like I carry a bit of Grandpa Frank by using my self-deprecating humour to build connections with others and point people to Jesus. There are good odds a sliver of what she has learned from me is something that will pass on to someone else and forever keep my legacy moving along.

Extra Auntie

My first pregnant friend
When I moved overseas
Let me hold her baby

My second pregnant friend
During my time in Germany
Told me there was an overflow of aunties

Years later a friend handed me
Her third child in infancy
"You can't keep her,"
Their firstborn told me

"Are you sure? She seems so happy with me."
She offered me her toddler brother instead.

When I prepared to move to another country
The parents laughingly offered the now pre-teen

The kid in her class
Who lived down the street
Called me Aunt Laura

There was an overflow of aunties
Then I moved to a new country

5

On Moving

I was a wreck when my family moved from my childhood home to the suburb just over during my fifth grade year of primary school. My mom was ready to have more than one bathroom with her family of four, and my sister was ready to have her own room (that was the biggest bonus for me too, to be fair). I saw a rare reflective side of my dad as we pulled away from the Park Way house.

"That might be the longest I've ever lived in any house," he commented.

I often forget that my dad was a military kid and moved around most of his life. I often forget my dad had a life before I came around. My students often forget I had a life before my accident.

Actually, that's a common motif with people I meet post-paralysis. They think, "You can pop a wheelie in that chair, so certainly it's inseparable from the rest of your history and identity."

When I move places now, I bring the chair with me. It moves me along. I've only moved like three times since my accident, and those moves were crossing international borders. I had only moved a couple of times after that significant move in elementary school before I packed up and loaded my life onto a jet across the Atlantic.

Some people live their whole lives in the same town, and I expected to be one of them. I loved the green rolling hills of my Portland suburb that was between the beach and the bustling hipster metropolis. I loved the familiarity of the view, particularly when I looked out from the comfy couch at Longbottom Coffee while sipping my large mocha.

I was happy in any coffee shop, even Starbucks. Sunday mornings always started with me showing up at the location next to Fred Meyers at Orenco. They knew me by order (which is more significant than knowing me by name) and would pour my fresh Venti drip the moment I walked through the door. It was waiting for me at the counter with the barista waiting for me to scan my phone app to deduct the amount from my gold card. I'd then add a splash of cream and a couple Splenda packets before retreating to the overstuffed chairs in the corner by the door. After reading my Bible and sipping the coffee for a bit, I'd take the rest of my Pike Place roast to Westport and get on with my day.

Westport Church was my home more than any place where I actually slept. I had people there who made the place my place. It was where I felt most known and most safe. I was able to be honest with people there, and they could call me out on my crap whenever necessary. Adults there saw my gifts and were actively developing me as a young leader starting as a teenager. Tina oversaw the handoff of responsibilities of running a growing children's ministry to me when I was barely twenty. Jen and Dave entrusted me with the leadership of the middle school small group while they were modelling leadership of the high school group.

Westport moved locations a couple of times in the early years, and each time we adjusted the space, we marked the moment as a point of growth in the church. Similar to most Third Culture Kids who grow up between cultures, the places I call home are marked by a combination of the place and the people as they connect to me with the emphasis on people over place. My dad has always struggled to understand why I never call any city in Colorado home. It's the strongest sense of home he has by place, but I've never lived there at any point in my life. The location is familiar to me, and many of the people I love most in the world — notably my two nephews — live there, but I've never spent more than a month of my life consecutively in that state. The place is not my home.

Portland is my heart's home in so many ways, but I haven't lived there in over a decade at this point, and I'm not sure whether I'll ever live there long-term again. Still, when I go back to visit, there's a return to my roots as I hop on the MAX line and wander the tree-lined streets filled with coffee shops, food carts, and environmentally conscious capitalists. The place is more home-like to me than Denver or Colorado Springs, but I feel most at home when my friends talk about the subtle nuances of coffee roasts — in a context that is not outrageous to be able to identify your favourite coffee bean blends.

"I'm with my people again! Did you know when I first moved to Germany, people thought I was pretentious because I could list my three favourite roasteries?"

"That's crazy; everyone can tell the difference between Sleepy Monk and Dapper & Wise and knows the latter is an upgrade."

"*Thank you!* And everyone knows that Starbucks makes the worst mochas because they use syrup, and you should only ever go to Black Rock or Dutch Bros for a mocha. Unless you can get to a Bella. They are the second best kind because they use powder. Or Ava's does it with real melted chocolate chips."

"Black Rock is far superior to Dutch Bros."

I legitimately had this conversation on a return visit to the Pacific Northwest in America. It actually went on for quite a while, and I was at home in that moment.

In Germany, I didn't usually drink German coffee. For the first several years, I had so many shipments of Longbottom and Stumptown beans as well as my strange Trader Joe's instant coffee taste of home items that I never needed to buy any local options to keep myself well caffeinated. In my third year teaching in Germany, a student discovered my appreciation for good coffee and began supplying me with Dominican coffee from his host country when he went back for breaks. He even mailed me some after he graduated. Drinking that Dominican coffee in my German apartment was just as much like tasting home as the TJs or Longbottom despite the disconnection from place for me.

A couple other students come from countries with good coffee, and we've shared stories of enjoying a good roast over the cheap, watered down or burnt tasting options we've encountered in different places. Different students would share their own expertise in consistency of gelato or spices in noodled cuisine when I listen to them reminisce about their "home." The demographic that I taught is a well-traveled lot who have likely called multiple countries home at some point in their young lives. Some of them are even fluent in three languages before puberty, and they show up in Germany with fresh eyes for the culture and look at how they can blend in as best as possible for their high school experience. I never had to deal with that kind of cultural competency in my monocultural upbringing, but I discovered the teenage tragedy covers all cultural bounds as these young people forged a home for themselves among the community of people in Kandern.

Moving overseas, I learned that my life was simultaneously unique from and exactly the same as the lives of my students. Returning to visit the place that raised me, I saw things with fresh eyes, and I remembered things I'd forgotten about the norms that I navigated with ease for the first twenty some years of my life.

I would never insist that moving and returning is a necessary growing experience for everyone, but for me, I've found countless benefits to being moved out of my complacency to see more of the world — one of which is to speak of others with greater empathy.

"Aren't you excited?" people would ask me all the time in the weeks leading up to my departure from America.

"No, I'm scared out of my pants."

I really was terrified of leaving my home for two years. At that point, I knew that it was a minimum commitment of two years, and that I wouldn't be visiting America for that duration. Two whole years. For a twenty-four year old, that seemed like a good chunk of time. Realistically, in the scheme of history, it's a blink, but I wasn't able to see that from my myopic life of comfort in the Pacific Northwest. Oregon is glorious and green. Why would I ever want to leave? My aunt had tried to convince me to move to Colorado Springs for a while, and I hated the thought of living in that brownish-red state for my whole life. It was dry and dying whereas my home state was lush and thriving.

The day I moved to Germany, my flight was out of SeaTac, a concession I was willing to make because it saved me several hundred dollars. One of my best friends, Sarah, had spent the night with me at my parents house to calm my nerves and came along with us on the long drive to the airport to see me off. Sarah had spent a semester in Kenya, so she knew about living away from America and all the culture shock that I was about to deal with as well as the minimalistic needs I would have. She actually spent hours with me the night before I left going through my three big suitcases and removing books to get me down to a much more reasonable and affordable two checked bags. At the time I packed them originally, it seemed really critical that I bring all my Elie Wiesel books and articles that I used to write my thesis. They were part of me, so how could I leave them behind? To her credit, Sarah didn't laugh in my face or slap me out of that stupidity. Instead, she calmly explained to me that I wasn't likely to write another thesis while I was teaching high school students, and the papers could all wait for me back in my parents' house.

The drive from Portland to SeaTac was familiar enough, and I didn't feel like I was leaving for anything particularly foreign as I looked out the windows at the I-5 traffic.

Sarah was still the level headed one when we checked into my flight and the mean airline employee changed up the rules I'd carefully read over and over about weight limits and carryon regulations. I was not going to be allowed to take my carryon and personal item despite the fact they were both under the listed weight regulations. Unruffled, Sarah selected items from my carryon to add to the checked bags until they each reached the max weight limit, and we pulled my computer out of my backpack to count that as my personal item and shoved items from my carryon bag into the backpack until it was as full as possible. My parents took the rest home with them and promised to mail it to me in Germany.

Due to my travel anxiety, I left plenty of time to make it through the security check point, and I found myself with even more time when my flight from Seattle to Frankfurt was delayed for an hour. I was sitting alone in the crowd of people waiting for the flight and decided to use my cell phone for the last time since it didn't have international coverage and would become a glorified iPod the moment I boarded the plane. I called another close friend to distract myself where I remember a deluge of nervous statements and questions.

"I can't believe I'm really doing this. Why aren't you with me? I'm freaking moving to Germany by myself. Weren't we supposed to be adventure buddies? What am I doing with my life? This is two whole years before I'll return to my passport country. Isn't this crazy? Should I really be doing this? It's too late to go back now. I mean, I could just not get on the plane, but, like, I paid for the ticket, and I'm here. So this is happening."

In reality, it was a conversation where my friend offered lots of calm and patient responses, and I wasn't exactly panicked, just on the verge of overwhelmed at the big move.

When I finally boarded the plane, I heard more German than English and immediately felt in over my head. At the time, I could only swear in German and didn't know any actually useful words. I found an angry German woman sitting in the aisle seat I'd reserved and had marked on my ticket. She refused to move, and I asked the flight attendant for help.

"That seat is empty, why don't you just sit there?" the flight attendant pointed to the middle seat of the middle section.

I climbed over two people and twisted my ankle to sit myself down in the cramped space. I didn't move from that spot for the next ten hours, and when I finally stood up, my leg almost gave way with the weight on my unhappy ankle. Hilariously, there are multiple mentions of this sore ankle in the first weeks of my journals in Germany. Just the day after arriving on foreign soil, I wrote, "I don't want my physical health to be a distraction for what you have prepared for my spiritual health," as I prayed that God would make my ankle feel better. Rereading those journal entries, I laugh as I think about how significant that barely noticeable limp was in the moment.

That first day in Germany was really wonderful, and the memory of the sore ankle isn't what stands out the most.

When I'd landed in Frankfurt, I had to run through the massive airport to make my connecting flight to Basel. Despite being in Germany, I was flying south and moving to a city close enough to the corner of a couple countries that the multi-national Basel airport was the best landing destination. They'd held up that short flight from Frankfurt to Basel because both my arriving plane from Seattle and another delayed plane arriving from Stockholm had passengers hoping to make this hop. Once I breathlessly boarded the tiny plane, we sat on the jetway for half an hour while waiting for the massive thunderstorm to lighten up enough for takeoff.

A staff member from Black Forest Academy named Dani was waiting for me at the French exit when I made it to the Basel airport. I felt immense relief when she stepped up to greet me, recognising me, I'm sure, from the combination of harried exhaustion and mild panic that accompanies newbies arriving in the BFA community for the first time. I'd been nervous about getting off the plane and loading into a car with someone I'd never met before. Dani had done the same with her husband a couple years before, and she was a pro at the international travel routine by the time I met her. She'd brought me a bottle of water and offered to let me drop my bags off at my new house before taking me out to dinner. She made international travel look easy. I had no idea how quickly I'd become that comfortable with the concept of international moves.

"Aren't you scared?" I heard repeated five years later in advance of my next international move.

"It's a whole lot less terrifying than the time I moved to Germany all by myself and hadn't met anyone there either. This time, I've at least got Chrissy coming with me for the flights. And it's not the first time I've flown over an ocean to live in a place where I've never met anyone. Last time, it worked out better than I could have dreamed. Why would this time be any different?"

Moving to New Zealand was a comparative breeze after the move from America to Germany. And I could walk on my own two feet without any mobility aids in that first move.

I learned a lot about moving in the five years I lived in Germany. I learned about how home really is a place tied to people, and I learned that you can never come back to a place exactly how you left it. I learned that life moves you around, and you make home as you move.

That last lesson came home hard after interacting with some Syrian refugees at a couple different points in my years in Germany. The first time I met refugees, it was a group of small children. I was asked to lead songs with the children while adults attended a service upstairs. I had the absolute delight of teaching twenty kids the motions to one of my favourite songs — "Jesus Soccer Star." I watched them dance along with smiles on their faces, and each one lit up when I pointed to them during the "I just came here to love *you*" line. As refugees in Germany, very few of those kids spoke English, so they had no idea what the song was about. We'd offered a summary of the song in German for the few who were learning the language of their new host country. I was so privileged as I led songs in that room because I had a home to call my own that I slept in that night.

I offered some behind the scenes help with that ministry a couple of times. I'll forever treasure the bright-eyed Syrian children who danced energetically around the tiny multipurpose room after we'd stacked the chairs up in the corner. They had that same unquenchable joy I saw in the two little Syrian girls who squirmed in my living room while their mom came over for tea a couple years later. I never expected any friendship with this woman, but my brief interactions with her have taught me a great deal about home.

We come from vastly different cultures. She sat in my home and described the literal war zone that she and her husband had fled with their children. They had come to Germany separately and only after several of their close family members had already been killed in the conflict. I listened to my new friend describe horrors of war that had touched her personally as tears filled her eyes before she abruptly told me, "And then I met you at the Rathaus in Kandern, and I saw God in your eyes."

Now it was my turn to tear up. I had no framework to understand why this woman and I were connected, but she told me she was now my

Syrian sister. We left our home countries for vastly different reasons, but we were now sisters brought together in Germany. She taught me the importance of finding family when moving from place to place. She knew I was living in a country without any blood connections, and she wanted to be sure to offer me a place in her family because the rest of mine was back in America.

About a week before I moved away from Germany for my year long totalisation, she came over for tea with two of her young daughters plus my friend Helen. We sat and listened to her describe the differences between Germany and Syria and some of her challenges adjusting to Western culture. Helen grew up in England, and I grew up in America, but we have different struggles that we found in our respective moves to Germany.

One thing that stood out to me was this woman's strong desire to return to Syria as soon as it was safe because so many of her extended family members were still there. Nothing in the world can substitute the rare moments I've had snuggling with my nephews, and I understand the pull. I've also embraced the fact that I'll live in a different country from my nephews for the majority of their lives, and I'll do the best I can to work with technology and time zones to be a part of their lives.

Lots of my students live in the dorms away from their parents, and they develop different strategies to stay connected with their families. I adjusted mine over the years as my sister's highly scheduled life clashes with my go-with-the-flow lack of routine in my non-work hours. Some students have the gift of easing into the moves that stretch the distance between them and their parents. Several dorm kids come from France or northern Germany where their parents are only a couple hours away by train, and they might even be able to visit on long weekends. Others can take up to two days of travel on planes, trains, and buses to get back to their parents' homes.

ON MOVING

A few of my students left a place they called home thinking they'd return during school breaks only to have their parents evacuated or relocated never giving the child a chance to say goodbye to the place. While some of the relocations are under duress or dangerous circumstances, others are natural moves as a ministry reassignment takes parents to another place. Audrey probably could never have prepared for her parents to leave Bulgaria, but she was particularly distraught to learn that her mom, dad, and three little brothers would not only be leaving her primary home behind, but they would be moving to Kandern, her secondary home, which would disrupt the concept of temporary home that she'd spent three years figuring out. Audrey actually really likes her family a lot; it was just going to confuse her ideas of school and not school homes. It was a lot for her to emotionally process. Tears were shed, and cookies were consumed in my kitchen.

This definitely wasn't the start of cookie making and crying at my house because Audrey was one of the few students who started tagging along with friends to my house before I even had her in class. The great respect she felt towards Maggie meant that when Maggie graduated, her word that I was a safe person was enough for Audrey to seek me out during the first emotional crisis of her second year of high school. I felt a mixture of dumbfounded and honoured as this worked up fifteen-year-old poured out her heart to me after a heated confrontation with a teacher who was not dealing with transition well. Raised respectful by Texan parents who taught her to both honour authority and value her own dignity, this champion responded to a staff member's inappropriate comment about her own difficult cross-cultural move to a class full of students by saying, "We do understand, ma'am, because we've done the same thing, and we're only fifteen." Then she left to go cry in the bathroom because she really didn't want to be disrespectful to this teacher but was overwhelmed by her emotions. She felt her own experiences of moving were being simultaneously ignored and expected as a mark of maturity in her life.

No one needs much time with Audrey to learn she feels everything deeply. She is fiercely loyal in her friendships because she cares for the people she is close to; she knows everything about the K-Pop group Stray Kids and thrives on learning every new song and all the details about the writing and recording process she can find. When her emotions get heightened, she'll start speaking Bulgarian. Once her gut gets words out in Bulgarian, her head can sort through her feelings in English. In the lead up to her parents' move, Audrey would sit at my picnic table wavering between the excitement of having her younger brothers close enough to hug regularly and the loss of access to things like authentic Bulgarian food.

"At least I can be one of the kids who comes back to visit you once I graduate now that my parents will live here too."

"I don't know how long I'm staying," I replied in all honesty.

One return visit was enough to look forward to at the time.

Because her parents moved mid-way through her senior year, and Audrey had already spent three and a half of her four years of high school in the same dorm called Storchenblick (Storch for short), there was a special arrangement for her to stay in the dorm while her brothers lived with her parents at home in town. Storch was her Kandern home, and there were particular places in Bulgaria that meant home to her as well. She had to grieve not being able to properly say goodbye to the Bulgarian places when her family packed up their belongings and drove their loaded van across the continent to join her in Germany. When her family moved, Bulgaria was still home in her heart, but it was forever changed for her future visits. She'd eventually get a trip with her mom to have quality closure with certain streets and shops, smells and sounds — a luxury not everyone gets when moving.

My moves have been blessed with the intentional endings and meaningful goodbyes. One of the hardest ones was my last family dinner with Audrey's family. A couple of weeks before her family relocated, Audrey had suggested I become part of weekly dinners at her parents' house once they settled in Kandern. Having only interacted briefly with her mom on a video call and messenger, I sent her a text that indicated I expected to have Fajita Fridays at her house once they moved. Absolute boss that she is, Stacie's reply was, "Can you even get fajita meat in Germany? Friday night is typically pizza and movie night for our family, but if I can get some good fajita meat, I'm open to it." I told her I was fine with pizza, and our friendship was sealed with a thumbs up gif. I spent nearly every Friday night having pizza and watching a movie with that family for the next year and a half. Once Audrey had gone off to college, I was teaching her oldest brother. Her youngest brother started calling me Aunt Laura. Audrey was visiting her family for the summer as I packed up the last of my life and belongings in Germany. I treasure those Friday nights with their whole family plus a few other stragglers around town they rounded up at their table.

A typical Friday in that season meant I'd show up around six to find Stacie still getting the pizzas ready. We'd chat in the tiny kitchen while I opened and closed the oven door when she needed to slide a tray in or out. Her husband or sons would come in and out joining the conversation or distracting the pizza process with questions that needed an immediate mom response. I was part of life in that place; I felt at home. The family had a routine shifting a chair away from the table to make space for my wheelchair, and I had my spot on the couch to transfer for the movie. If I said I needed to leave early, I might get home by half past nine, but more likely I'd be wheeling home around midnight.

Door to door was just a few minutes, but I'd savour the journey, slowing down before turning onto the gravel in front of my house and looking up at the sky either littered with stars and a bright phase of the moon or the tall branches of the walnut tree criss-crossing the thick clouds. I'd take a deep breath in the quiet cold and thank God for this place I lived, for where I moved to, knowing in a corner of my soul I'd someday move from it too.

Stacie was one of the very first people I told about the job opportunity in New Zealand. Her face was gravely serious when she told me I would have to be the one to inform her youngest son — the one who calls me Aunt Laura — that I'd be moving. He wasn't the kid who took it the hardest though. Across an ocean, Audrey had another emotional crisis as she realised I was not going to be in her home place in any future visits after that coming summer.

We spent a lot of time together during her long visit, and she helped me with loads of the packing and cleaning and details of my move, but it wasn't easy for her. Audrey will always be in my life in some way, and I treasure knowing that no matter where either of us moves in the future, we will be a piece of home for each other.

6

On Hospitality

According to my dad, every Sunday lunch in his childhood home was like a Thanksgiving feast as his parents invited stragglers and strangers into their home to enjoy hospitality at their table. My dad's memory of my grandma is as a cooking magician who happened to cover every vegetable with cheese to get her husband and kids to eat it but who also shared the love of Christ through her table as she filled plates and hearts.

There was a bit of an ache that my dad could never fill when his wife and daughters lacked the same passion for weekly feasts at home. My mom passed on a different kind of hospitality to me, however, and I've landed on some amalgamation in the end. Rather than filling stomachs, my mom made space for hearts to open up around her; she also chose to do it in coffee shops or office chats or catch ups between carpools rather than at her own dining table. Between the stories and my lived experience, I learned the value of hospitality. What really mattered was making space for people in your life; the food was less important.

I did develop a love for baking, though, and I loved how my parents let me invite my entire high school to my birthday party at our house when I turned sixteen. I had loads of cupcakes ready as a wide range of my peers showed up on Super Bowl Sunday despite the fact I told them we weren't watching the biggest game of the National Football League season. It ended up on the TV anyways, and I embraced the mistake in the following few years to host a "Super Birthday Bowl" where people from every corner of my life came over whether or not they liked American football. The game was on in one room, and I was always hanging out and playing Apples to Apples in the other room. We sang "Happy Birthday" and handed out cupcakes during halftime.

Without my parents purposefully doing it, our house was a hub of hospitality for my friends in high school and university. My mom always made sure our house was spotless, and I always made sure to leave some mess around so people would realise real humans lived in this place. Despite my sloppy style, my mom cared more about people feeling loved than she did about their judgement of her clean home. I should note, if you know my mom, that's saying something because she really does weirdly care that her house is spotless for other people — she just loves people feeling loved *that much more*. My dad also loves people in his home because he just loves people being around constantly. He's incredibly extroverted. My mom and I are incredibly introverted, and our willingness to host anything is a testament to our devotion to Jesus more than anything else.

Examining my mom's struggle to open her home reveals some interesting things about my outlook on being made in the image of God. You see, I know my mom pretty well, and she would never, ever suggest hosting things at her home, especially if she has to cook or bake, but countless people have received generous hospitality from my mom. Genuine, heartfelt, open, loving hospitality. When it happens to be in my mom's house, I guarantee you, she asked my dad not to do it, but he convinced her it was worth it, and in the end, after some stress and anxiety, my mom had no regrets over welcoming people in. But she will never suggest it.

She'd suggest a follow up one-on-one conversation with each person, and her preference would be to drive through Dutch Bros and pick up a drink for you before she met you at your house or a public place that she didn't have to clean. She'd have a pack of tissues on hand or a big box in her car as a back-up because she's prepared to hear whatever is on your heart right then. She's got a load of life experience that she won't be quick to share, but once you've spent a couple hours pouring your jumbled thoughts and feelings out, she will offer you a nugget of wisdom that fits your situation. Then she will file away every detail that you told her, keep it locked confidentially in her brain, and follow up with you the next time you have a heart to heart. That's just how she functions.

My dad won't remember your name, but he'll recognise your face, consider you family, and ask when you can bring your whole family — kids, cousins, and uncles included — over for dinner at his house. He'll probably promise that my mom will cook. If you haven't made it to my parents' house for a meal yet, I promise it's not because my dad hasn't wanted you; it's most likely that there's a waiting list because my mom does need some introvert recharge time and can't host every night without a break like my dad wants. He loves people so genuinely that he wants to have more contact points; my mom loves people so genuinely, she wants deeper contact points. Call it a quantity versus quality tension if you like.

There might be a fight between my parents about how to show hospitality specifically, but the thing is, they're so aligned on the Gospel and extending kingdom hospitality in general that they've stayed together for over forty years now. They both embody this thing about the human need for connection, and they've lived out a strong ethic of reaching out to others through whatever means are available and most natural to their personalities. Not only that, but they showed me that living out the Gospel sometimes means living outside of our comfort zones.

Throwback to my first Super Birthday Bowl: I was actually really upset about the game ending up on the TV. I'd made plans to watch my favourite movies, and I'd told everyone before showing up that we wouldn't be watching the Super Bowl. The crowd of people was there to celebrate my birthday, and I was devastated when it became about a football game instead of me. I snuck upstairs and cried in my room by myself for half an hour. Once my tantrum was over, I still had a great birthday. By the next year, I made the most of the NFL timing and created something where a range of people could enjoy themselves — not just the anti-football people like me. I was thrown way out of my comfort zone in that party atmosphere, but I saw how people from all contexts of my life were engaged and connecting with each other.

Those years I hosted a Super Birthday Bowl party became a beautiful tradition as I welcomed church friends, school friends, peers, adults, kids, and people I'd met that morning to my family's house. One year I invited a visitor from church, and he showed up and had a blast meeting all my friends. Another year a close family friend met a girl I knew from youth group and discovered she was likely a distant cousin because of the unique spelling of her last name. My dad thrived on all the different people in the house, and my mom would eventually settle down from cleaning. I didn't particularly notice the kingdom values on display through those annual events because it was just the norm of my upbringing. People were welcome in our home.

When I moved out in grad school, I was thrilled with the first opportunity to fill my car with my small group girls and bring them to my apartment. They broke my heating unit the only night it snowed that year, but I still loved the chance to have ice cream sundaes in winter with those goofy teenagers who made themselves at home in my apartment. Those moments of hospitality in my home space were infrequent in grad school due to my schedule. More often, my spare moments were in comfy coffee shop chairs listening to my small group girls or the heart friends I held onto after high school. I still had my Super Birthday Bowl party at my parents' house those six years though.

Moving to Germany was yet another shift of furniture and hospitality mindset. I didn't have enough time to find routines before my accident, but once I moved into my apartment in the building we called the "HammerHouse," I knew I wouldn't be having many dinner parties. At least, I thought I wouldn't be able to. The collection and arrangement of furniture when I first moved in didn't have a dining table, and the small table squeezed awkwardly into the kitchen space could barely fit food for two people and was super tight the times I tried to feed a third. I was somewhat resigned to this as I started inviting young people over for tea. They could sit comfortably on my couch and put their mugs on my side tables. Two, three, up to five could squeeze on the seating available and have a cup of tea.

When we added baking into the after-school mix, teenagers would mingle in my kitchen, sitting on the window counter, the two chairs squeezed at the table, or in various corners on the floor. By the time I started hosting dinner for dorm kids at my house, I knew they'd be comfortable on the floor even if I felt that was a bit below the standards I'd like to offer.

An absolute game changer happened once I returned from New Zealand. The four years I'd lived in the HammerHouse before my sabbatical, we had a rotting picnic table in the shade between two trees. While I was gone, a storm knocked down one tree, and the landlord decided it was time to upgrade the table. By the time I returned, it was a year old, but it was new to me. I loved this picnic table. It was beautiful and, well, there. Presence. That picnic table is a huge part of my story now, and it's a formative place in the stories of countless young people who crossed my path at that place and encountered the Holy Spirit.

One friend identified it as what the Celtic Christians call a "thin place." Anytime a young person would ask me about my magic table, I would explain to them the idea of the thin place. Celtics believed there were certain locations on earth that were just easier to encounter God in. They weren't actually magic places, but they were places that people frequently reported hearing the Holy Spirit or feeling the presence of God in powerful ways. Usually they were somewhat random places in nature. However, some Christians realised that if they had particular prayer places that they'd prayed in for a decade, then it was sometimes easier to hear God there. Others found the same effect in a location that other warriors of the faith had prayed in often. I have some theories about when and how my picnic table became a thin place, but whatever the catalyst, this place became a magnet for teenagers seeking hospitality.

My first year with the table, students started inside the house, but when Covid hit that spring, they couldn't come in anymore. Our gatherings were forced to the table as well as to shrink in size. Shockingly, when the German regulations were most stringent through the winter and we couldn't have more than two households gathered together and had to be spaced out, my picnic table picked up traction. Young people would come in pairs and sit on the bench outside my window in the literal snow as I opened the window in my entryway and let them warm their hands on the radiator. I did my best to honour the spirit of the regulations while meeting the craving for hospitality these isolated young people had. They wanted to be somewhere with people, and I could pass them a cup of tea through the window and keep the fresh air moving in my entryway. When the temperature lifted, we spaced four people at the corners, and when the regulations lifted, we crammed as many bums on those benches as possible.

As soon as school started in the fall of 2021, the seniors were gathering at my table after school. The first week, a group filled up the spaces at the table, the girls from Palmgarten dorm bringing along their new senior sister who hadn't taken my class the past year. A couple of home students lingered, and a few funny stories were shared about some of the people seated at the table. After we all laughed at one particularly hilarious story from a notoriously good humoured girl, I suggested we all share something kind about her character. It wasn't contrived; honestly, it fit the moment as we laughed about a mistake she'd made and all knew she was one of the sweetest, most inclusive, kind, and compassionate girls in her grade. Her eyes filled with tears as she listened to her peers list the positive character attributes they saw in her. I was thrown by the emotional response, and when she managed to choke out that she'd never heard those kind of nice things about herself, I insisted we go around the table and hear affirmations of everyone. We took our time and said purposeful truths about these precious young people. A student from the Maugenhard dorm texted her dorm parents that she'd be late for dinner because she didn't want to miss the chance to say affirmations to her friends. This had become a holy moment and would change the trajectory of their senior year as this group intentionally shifted how they spoke to one another.

There was a ripple effect as more kids showed up at my house expecting tears and affirmations. There weren't tears every time, but that new girl joked with me midway through the year about how the first three times she showed up at my house she and her friends all ended up crying. "I just associate crying with coming to Ms. Hewett's now," she laughed. When I invited all the Palmie seniors over for dinner in February, they insisted we each write sticky note affirmations for each other person. Her note to me included that detail about people crying while pointing out that she kept coming back because she felt welcome at my house. Another one of her dorm sisters who had just arrived that year and not taken my class had a similar sentiment as she said she felt safe showing up at my house.

One of the things that struck me through that year was what a low bar it was for me to sit at my picnic table and say kind things to students. I enjoy baking, so I had more than enough to share, and I made it my personal goal to bake allergy friendly options for the celiac and special diet kids because I knew how many treats I'd missed out on growing up.

Well before the first affirmation session and the norm of gluten free goodies at my house, one of the celiac students stopped by on his way home from school and perched on my bench while I sat at my open entry window. Jacob took my class in the fall of 2020 which was during the height of Covid regulations, and he'd just moved back to Germany after a year in America for his parents' totalisation. His brothers had been able to have all their high school years in Germany uninterrupted, and it was pretty hard for Jacob to leave the friends and town he'd known since early elementary school for this single year away before returning for the last two years of high school. A global pandemic didn't help.

Jacob poured out his life story that September afternoon and gave me the privilege of watching his faith grow through the coming years. I remember thinking in the moment how odd it was that he was sharing all this information with me. Who was I to receive this gift of his story? Every time someone chooses to be vulnerable and share their life experiences, it's an honour. This particular kid is your poster child good kid: clean and tidy, respectful and responsible, high achieving academically and all around involved in extra-curricular activities. He's also complex and has a fragile history of insecurity and depression while simultaneously being quick witted and cheeky with a compassion that runs so deep he'd mow his elderly landlady's lawn for free. He'd even eat her gluten filled treats and listen to her stories knowing he'd be in gastrointestinal distress later but too polite to turn down her generosity and need for company. While I went out of my way to bake gluten free options, I am confident that he never would have told me if I accidentally made him sick with my food. He'd just smile broadly and keep eating whatever I offered him.

Jacob spent a lot of time in my classroom and at my table over the next two years. While I usually had *brötchen* for lunch that would have made him sick, I routinely made gluten free goodies to have on hand for Jacob and his friends who would gather at my table.

They didn't come for the snacks.

This is a significant hospitality side note: people aren't craving appetisers, salads, and casseroles so much as they are craving welcome, belonging, and community.

At the start of Jacob's senior year, just days before the first impromptu affirmation gathering, a long line of student council and worship team members walked past my house on their way to school with their staff sponsors. Approximately three quarters of the young people diverted to my table to give me a hug; I happened to have brownie bites on the table and offered them up. A new staff member saw the interaction and told me the next day she loved the baking ministry I had.

"Wha—?" I floundered, not knowing what she was referring to. I'd offered her and her husband cookies every day on their way to and from new staff orientation, and they'd turned down both the baked goods and any conversation with me each time. She told me she saw how students flocked to my table for the baked goods.

"Ooooh," I nodded and didn't elaborate.

What she had misunderstood was that the kids came with or without the baked goods. The food was a reason to invite adults, my peers, to the table. Young people didn't need the pretence, but they ate my food when it was on the table. Over the next couple of years, she would build strong rapport with many of the BFA kids and learn they would connect with adults without being fed by them. Her comment says something to me about a wider understanding of hospitality though. My home, my place, my picnic table, was a space where students felt loved, seen, and accepted. They felt heard, known, and affirmed. Like I said, this picnic table became a magnet for students, and I wasn't doing anything. I'd come home to students waiting for me in pairs and clusters, or I'd be sitting on my couch and hear a knock on my front window (for some reason they never used the doorbell) when students wanted to hang out on a Saturday.

My neighbours in the building were totally in on it, and we shared life at that table through lots of seasons. Anna would sit out there and read her Bible. Amanda would read *The Lord of the Rings* aloud to Emily and I stretched out on the table. Aly or Emily or Lauren would join me for a glass of wine while we stargazed at night. Lauren would have her off-campus meetings at the table after dragging it into the shade. In different years, David and Dustin would bring their coffee down and watch their youngest kids run around our dirt by the table. Hannah would bring out her breakfast to enjoy it in the sunshine on good weather days. So many meals covered that table, but it was hearts that were filled as Hammer-House residents hosted and shared life in that space.

I felt it a privilege to host so many of the gatherings as other people entered that holy ground. Some of my students would tell me they felt different when they crossed the property line; call it a thin place activation or a God thing or whatever you like. This place wasn't ordinary once ordinary people gathered in the name of Jesus. That's all that was happening. Jesus followers showed up consistently to sit at that table with a cup of coffee or a brownie bite or a gluten free pumpkin chocolate chip oatmeal cookie. Or just their stories and a listening ear and compassion for others.

Soon after I was offered the job in New Zealand, I was offered nearly an apartment's worth of furniture that could be stored until my arrival several months later. Included in the mix was a large dining table with eight chairs. As I began praying for the home I'd move into, I asked God for a place where I could host others. I'd loved the culture I'd begun to cultivate as students and peers felt welcome in that picnic table space. I also lamented not being able to squeeze many people inside when the weather was cold. I'm writing this chapter from the living room that has already comfortably hosted nearly twenty people in one go. I've had multiple planned and impromptu gatherings as I share baked goods with friends and young people. I've had a table to host meals at for some invited in advance and others brought along unexpectedly after church. I love that I'm able to open my doors and feed people but most importantly that I can share hospitality even when my pantry is running low.

One of the beauties of kingdom hospitality that is beyond food is that you get to receive just as much as you give when you cultivate this habit. The life on life I shared with people at my table was often a mutual blessing. Sure, some of it was the hard work of ministry like when I was woken up from a nap by banging at my kitchen window because some kids wanted a cookie and a cup of tea and a piece of my humanity. When the Palmies asked to relocate their traditional senior Valentine's Day dinner outing to be at my house because the Covid regulations wouldn't allow them to go to a restaurant, it sounded like an ordeal I didn't want to commit to. However, what they further explained was that the tradition was the seniors bonding and that they wanted to come to my house because that was a place they felt safe and loved and where they could have a positive experience. By that point it wasn't a surprise they chose to make the night's big activity writing affirmations to one another. Plus dancing with my cardboard cutout of Daveed Diggs.

I may not make a Thanksgiving feast each Sunday lunch, but I am always on the lookout for stragglers who need a meal. I also generally have tissues on hand in case people start crying around me (which still happens far more than I expect). When the senior youth group leaders asked if they could plan a movie night at my house this week, I didn't hesitate. I'm not cooking a meal for them which instantly makes it easier, but honestly, I would have if they'd asked. I've grown into this form of hospitality that will happily cultivate connections because whatever it means to be made in the image of God, it has to do with relationship.

I stand by that statement, as introverted as I am, so I'll plan accordingly to recharge as necessary and engage wholeheartedly in the moments I'm given to love other people well.

7

On Community

"I know there are loads of people who would take a bullet for you in Kandern, Laura, but I've never heard you talk about community here the way you do with the church in New Zealand."

The words stung with how true they rang as Alyssa and I processed the way I'd been sidelined, excluded, and hurt by the "community" I lived in for ten years. My friend Hannah who's a native Kiwi was the one who suggested I write a chapter on community to round out the manuscript I was editing.

I grappled with the implications of what might come out in a chapter on community when I really loved and valued so many individuals in the *Dreiländerek*, that tiny corner of Europe where I made so many connections and found support to grow in my faith for a long season of life. Having lived on three continents and wrestled with feelings of marginalisation before and after a physical disability, I wondered where I might accidentally hurt people in sharing the ways they'd accidentally hurt me. But maybe that needs to happen so we can all learn some ways to heal past wounds and prevent future hurts among our neighbours. Full of my human imperfections, I'll give this chapter some of my honest reflections from a few of the scars and some of the tender happy moments of living amongst people of God.

When I look at stories of people who have lifelong bonds with the friend group they went to high school with, I marvel at the beauty. I don't have that kind of story. I have a handful of people who I went to high school with who I loosely keep in touch with, but none of them are close to me, and I haven't lived on the same continent as any of them for over a decade. I did develop a different bond of community when I was in university however, and those tight friends first found me as a high school junior. When I joined Westport as a church plant just after getting a drivers' license, I was put in a small group with Sarah and Rachel who were both students at Multnomah. They'd have a significant influence on the trajectory of my education as well as my spiritual and social life. I'd also became close to their roommate Jordyne who didn't attend Westport with us but occasionally joined our late-night movie adventures after stressful Sundays.

Sarah is a movie buff, and she was horrified to discover that I'd reached nineteen years of age without ever seeing *The Breakfast Club* or *RENT*. She and Rachel insisted upon fixing this. Simultaneously, we hatched a plan to get up to an adventure that could let the staff and elders of our church know that they were loved and appreciated. We wanted them to feel loved, not vandalised, so we purchased bouquets of flowers along with lots of toilet paper, plastic forks, and streamers.

Young as we were, we didn't require much sleep, so we spent a few hours watching movies and letting our loved ones go to sleep before leaving the east side where Sarah and Rachel lived and spreading love across the west side where all the Westport leadership resided. Trusting my confidence that Krispy Kreme was open 24 hours, we didn't pre-load on sugar before we drove across Portland at 1am. We were all disappointed to discover my error as the lights were all off at the only Oregon location at the time, so we drove into Hillsboro with adrenaline alone.

Sarah, Rachel, and I hit up like eight houses and Shannon's apartment door. To my knowledge, I was involved in every subsequent Westport tping event as well, but nothing tops that first night when the three of us stayed out all night trying not to laugh too hard as we tossed the toilet paper rolls into trees and stabbed cheap disposable cutlery in lawns before leaving flowers on the doorstep of people we loved and respected.

Once we crossed the bridge to the east side again, we were laughing hard, and I felt so light hearted as we settled onto the couch for the last movie before we went to sleep. Jordyne came in at some ridiculous hour which should have seemed strange but didn't after the three of us had just showed our affection for our church leadership by littering on their lawns. It was joy upon joy as I got to spend time with two of my favourite people while offering a token of affection to other people I considered significant in that season of my life.

Jordyne wasn't involved in that toilet papering, but she was involved in lots of other shenanigans the four of us got up to. During a particularly hard season of life, Sarah and Rachel were picking me up at the end of youth group on the west side and driving me back across town to my dorm in North Portland. They had a ministry commitment nearby where I was serving and would drop me at my dorm before going to their apartment. Though I can't confirm the number, in my memory, most Sunday nights we'd detour to a cheap movie theatre near my university and catch a ten or eleven PM showing of whatever comedy was out at the time. We weren't watching high quality films, but we were laughing our heads off to destress the other things out of our control in life. Usually we'd text Jordyne what time the movie showing was, and she'd meet us there. Since our routine was to head there after youth group, we'd often be the only ones in the theatre and waiting twenty minutes or more for a movie to begin.

One night Jordyne and I sat next to each other chatting while Sarah and Rachel were in the bathroom or getting snacks. We joked it would be really funny to hide from them in the theatre. With no good spots available in the rows of chairs, we laid ourselves down on the floor. It's important to note that Jordyne is the biggest germaphobe I've ever met in my life, and I'm not far behind her in my disgust of being dirty. Within seconds we realised the error of our ways, but we were committed to the bit. Once Sarah and Rachel walked back in, they spotted us immediately, and before we could even ask, one of them commented, "You can't go home and shower until after the movie's over." I obviously survived the character-building experience of sitting in clothes that were sticky from unknown years of movie snacks and drinks spilled on that theatre floor. That story reflects so much of our impromptu hijinks that held so much joy without any of the ramifications I watch other twenty-somethings deal with when they do dumb stuff. I think often of how those three friends adventured through life with me in wild and crazy circumstances, being silly but never stupid and always pointing me towards Jesus. I road tripped across America with them multiple times, and just a couple years after I moved to Germany, Jordyne flew over for Christmas and stayed a month until Sarah and Rachel could come spend a week with us as well and have a mini road trip across Europe. On one of our long adventures, I remember sitting in a hotel room with them and confessing that I was always worried I'd be kicked out of the friend group because I was the baby (they're all a couple years older than me), and maybe they only thought of me as a hanger-on who they couldn't get rid of.

"Laura, that's ridiculous," Rachel told me matter of factly, "We've put far too much effort into raising you to get rid of you. You're stuck in this friend group."

I then got some behind the scenes reflections on the first time Sarah had hung out with me and told Rachel afterwards how annoying she thought I was. Rachel told her they had to give me a chance to grow up, and eventually I did.

Rachel was also the one to share some significant insight with me on what deep friendship means and looks like when I was musing on how hard it was to make friends when I first moved to Germany. "I don't think most people have what we do," she told me before sharing about some new friends she'd made who didn't have the life-on-life, soul-on-soul connection our forged family had. On the one hand, I felt a little bit better about my struggle to make deep connections with people in Germany, but I also saw the craving for more with lots of the young adults and families in transition in and out of that foreign missionary community.

The nebulous social security treaty situation between countries only complicated life for those who wanted to put down some roots and build community in Kandern while serving on missionary visas. People had to live life with six-year cycles of a full year disrupting patterns in Germany to be outside of the country for 366 days after five full years in one place. Extensions could be granted for a couple of years, but you would have to plan around which child's schooling to disrupt when and who else was going to be gone the year before or after you. Some friendships might be on face to face pause for two years while you alternated who was away.

When the second season of *Stranger Things* came out, the perfect analogy clicked into place as I reflected on the social tension involved in making and maintaining friendships in the particular transitory international community that is Kandern, Germany. For those unfamiliar, in season one of this thriller series, a tight friend group of four boys lose one friend to "the upside down" and befriend a new girl (who happens to have super powers). In season two, Will comes back from the upside down and is frustrated with how this new girl, Eleven, has usurped some of his friendships. She's confused by him asserting closeness to the people she's bonded with over the past year without him. The rest of the boys are navigating their close bonds with both Will and Eleven each while wanting to knit those two together. Then you throw the new girl Max in who has just moved to town and wants to join the friend group. Everyone is new to her, and she's unaware of the social tensions that are reintegrating Will back in and Eleven learning her place with Will restored.

My first year in Kandern was filled with stories of staff who'd be returning in a year while I found my place among returners and those who'd been around a while. Then I had my year outside the town and had the awkwardness of reintegration to a new bunch of people who had spent the year I was away learning the ropes of the school and social networks. As I fit back in and knew deeper channels of how to get things done, I accidentally ruffled few feathers amongst new staff who didn't know my history among the old guard around the school. Messy is an understatement as I found my place and worked hard to include others who were waffling on the edges of something called a community.

Making deep friendships and finding the people you connect with is emotionally exhausting, and I want to emphasise that as I say how many of the people who were long-term residents of Kandern were relationally burned out from losing so many close friends. I became one of those burnt-out individuals myself after about four years — which was around the time I found more than one family who would adopt me and provide the familial bond I needed to not feel isolated the majority of the time.

During my year away, I found myself in a church *whānau* that was made up of many families who'd been around the church for decades and a thriving young adult ministry that purposefully integrated university students into church life. This certainly isn't a perfect community, but the Māori concept of *whānau* goes a long way among these people to create a familial bond that is more than a Sunday morning smile. I was wrapped up in community here on the basis of a friend of a friend saying I needed somewhere to stay on sabbatical. When I headed back to

Kandern, I purposefully looked for how I could be better at finding people on the margins and connecting with them. To be honest, a huge part of my motivation was to recreate what I'd experienced in New Zealand, and a significant portion of my soul longed to go back to that *whānau* in Christchurch for good. I obviously jumped at the opportunity when God opened the door for me to return. I had zero hesitation to apply for the job and figure out the complicated visa process because I knew there were people waiting for me to return.

After over twenty-four hours of travel from Kandern to Christchurch in August 2023, I finally made it through the customs with my bags to find my friend Haley waiting for me with a jar of marmite to welcome me home. Home. What a messy word, but as soon as I wheeled through the airport doors and towards the carpark, I said it out loud to Haley: "I'm home." It was so satisfying.

After nearly a year back in Christchurch, someone asked me casually in conversation, "Where's home for you?"

"Well, that's a complicated question," I answered honestly, "Here is the most home to me, in Christchurch, but I moved here after ten years of living in Germany which became a home, but I grew up in the Pacific Northwest of America, in Portland, Oregon." It's a mouthful to get through, but omitting any of those homes would be a disservice to my heart's sense of place. Even more accurately in my mind, however, home is more food and people than it is place. Home is Haley hugging me before she hands me the jar of marmite to welcome me back. Home is going out to brunch with Alyssa and Bethany, home is lounging at my picnic table with Lissy or Chris eating fresh baked goods, home is late night drinks with Emily and Robbie, home is mozzarella sticks with Givorgy and Bekah, home is watching cheesy movies with Shannon while eating pizookie. Home is spicy shrimp pasta and cheesecake with Esther.

Given the opportunity, I would have Esther Kim make me spicy shrimp pasta for dinner every night. I wouldn't want to make it all on my own, but I would need my precious alumni to take over my kitchen, fight with my chilli flakes, and tell me about all the current drama in her life. And then I would want to fill my table with a rotation of people from across the continents who have had influence or insight in my life. Esther would be a staple for the way she's taught me about community through sharing food in particular.

During her second year of university, Esther was doing a study abroad year in Freiburg, but still knowing several staff and students, she would come visit Kandern every couple of weeks. More often than not, she would sleep on my pullout couch. If ever possible, I'd get her to cook or bake for me because she is far more talented than I am with her culinary experiments. Early on in the year, she wanted to try a shrimp pasta recipe at my house. Despite my seasonings fighting her, she managed to create a delicious masterpiece. Whenever she returned, if there was going to be a meal at my house, we aimed to have shrimp pasta. Several times she invited other people over to join in, but even if it was just us, I'd insist upon the shrimp pasta.

Eventually, we had a running joke about how both of us, particularly me, ate pasta constantly. She would begin tagging me in pasta memes on Facebook, and more often than not, I'd be eating pasta when I read it. Like Sophia Loren, when you look at my body, everything you see is thanks to spaghetti. It was more than buttered noodles in my own kitchen though, and with Esther around, she made sure there was a good kick with the generous amounts of chilli flakes.

I read a book recently that said people will eat more healthy if they are sharing meals with others. I know that I was healthier when I was sharing meals with Esther because I spent a solid two hours laughing while she was making the food. Laughter is great exercise for your abdomen. I'm sure I would have washboard abs if I hired her as my full time cook. Even if she made me shrimp pasta every night. There are also loads of statistics about the higher resilience and mental health strength of young people who have families who eat meals together regularly.

Sharing food is sharing community. When I invited Esther in for the night, we ended up sharing life, and it was a beautiful expression of the body of Christ when she baked me a birthday cheesecake because she heard it was my favourite dessert and made a special trip down to visit me the weekend before my birthday knowing I'd be gone on the day. It was also a special taste of heaven when she would come and bring her left over chocolate chip cookies from stress baking before exams and we would settle in on my couch while matching the traits of the cast of *The Goonies* to her brother and his four closest friends. It's easier to bond when baked goods are involved, and you share a special connection with people when you share a meal.

After Esther's first cheesecake, several other students asked for the opportunity to make me a cheesecake. I generally provided the space, the ingredients, and the *Mean Girls* Broadway soundtrack, but the students did all the work of making the dessert. By the end of the year, I'd had six cheesecakes specially made for me or at least shared with me. I savoured each unique one, but nothing really topped Esther planning out how to get me my favourite dessert and sharing it with me on the closest possible day to my birthday that she could see me.

Esther and I each enjoyed the tasty dessert, but it wasn't until she was leaving at the end of the weekend that I actually realised she'd come down just to see me. Esther is a beloved student with no shortage of friends, and when she asked to come for the weekend, I assumed she wanted to spend time with some of the current students more than with her old Bible teacher. The food was an excuse to see me.

Each of us is hungry for connection with people, and food is a conduit to community that I can't dismiss. They aren't a whole picture though, which is what Alyssa was getting at when she told me she'd never heard me talk about community like I did when I described my church in New Zealand. Haley picked me up from the airport and took me to my favourite coffee shop to get a caffeine kick and some banana bacon pancakes to keep me fuelled up enough to last until the evening and shared with me that the day my return was announced in church was the day her son was dedicated in service. We shared excitement about me getting to watch him grow up and to eventually shepherd him through youth group. He's come over with her to hang out at my house a couple of times, and he associates the street they turn off to get to mine with coming to have chocolate and tea with me.

I joined a life group with young kids included, and one of them frequently draws me pictures or makes crafts to give me. My collection is growing across my home and office. We also do a Bible story and prayer time with the kids during life group, and one of the first weeks, I was so incredibly touched to listen to a young boy praying for my physical healing. He's had lots of conversations with his mom about my disability and how he still sees so much joy in me but is learning that we are asking for God to restore my ability to walk so that I can have even more joy. We're teaching another kid that the anti-tip bar on the back of my wheelchair is for the jet rockets, so he can't touch it. These families share the serious and the silly with me.

I love getting to do life on life with these people and know any one of them will give me a ride home if it's too dark for me to wheel or if I want to take my crutches and can't make it independently.

A Note on Tenses

I am a teacher
A decade in a classroom
New Title; New Place:

I stayed a teacher
But my classroom looks different
Writing these words now

Bear with me as a break the form a bit
Bear with me as I shift and change the look

The slant rhyme hitting fine
Or the meter marching to a different beat

When you read my thoughts
I wrote them as a teacher
Past or present tense

8

On Teaching

Former teacher turned slam poet Taylor Mali has a great spoken word poem called "What Teachers Make." It's told as a response to a lawyer trying to denigrate the profession of education, and one of my favourite lines is, "You want to know what I make? I make kids work harder than they ever thought they could." People tend to think of the job of a teacher in either incredibly lofty terms or as a cop-out career. Considering the fact that I am a teacher by trade, I think it's probably clear where my bias lies.

I don't know if I'd go so far as to say it's the greatest profession, but it's certainly critical to the thriving of a culture and arguably a healthy economy. I'm less concerned about those things though; teaching is critical to the thriving of healthy individuals. I was incredibly fortunate to have a series of wonderful teachers from preschool through university. I interacted with people who saw me as an individual worth investing in because I was a unique human created in the image of God. I had a couple less-than-stellar teachers thrown in the mix too, but overall, the impression I got was that most of these people genuinely cared about me learning their content because it would benefit me as a person.

As a professional educator, I read a lot about best practices and how to be a good teacher. One of the more surprising statistics is that the best teachers aren't necessarily focused on their students as individuals but rather have an unwavering devotion to their content which then inspires their students to engage and achieve. I can't argue with the research, but I can speculate about what might be missing in the conclusions.

I care a whole lot about my content. During my first semester at BFA, I was teaching English literature and a Bible elective. All my students knew I was a part of both departments and that I loved teaching both. Just before Christmas, I was wrapping up studying *A Christmas Carol* with my ninth graders. Most Americans watch some version of the movie every year, but it was less familiar to the majority of my TCKs who all grew up living among multiple cultures, so I got a little excited when we reached the end and saw the turnaround in Scrooge from a miserly grouch to a loving benefactor to those in his sphere of influence.

"How would you live differently if you genuinely embraced the lavish grace you have been given by God to be generous to others? What would you do if you had the chance to make a difference in someone's life? Would you just wish them well and return to your comfort, or would you look for ways to extend the love of God to them? Jesus talks about this when he says we will one day be told we either extended love to him or rejected him in the form of our kind deeds to the poor and oppressed."

I may have gotten a little carried away in my excitement, but I had a rapt audience of fourteen-year-olds. They listened quietly, and when I finally took a breath at the end, one student cautiously said, "Wow, I can see why you really like teaching Bible class."

"Are you *kidding me*? This is why I love teaching *English class!*"

When I was in university, one of my English professors used to frequently talk about how the purpose of literature is to develop empathy in the readers. A different professor wrote a book on how to read the Bible which claims the whole purpose of reading the Bible is to foster loving relationships with God and other people. A third professor connected the dots for me that reading well was significant in how I lived out my faith because the texts should change me — for the better. And the Bible should change me most of all.

Literature excited me because it was an avenue to develop how I read the Bible, but it also was a way to practice empathy and to grow as a person. I had wanted to be an English teacher since my second year in high school, and I was only more entrenched in that conviction through my university years as I learned more about good teaching. I had been inspired by plenty of my teachers along the way, and I was pursuing a career that allowed me the opportunity to inspire future students.

So I do care about my content — a great deal — but I connected it to the individuals that came through my classroom. I can teach Bible or English and be passionate about the texts I'm presenting to the room, but it's my conviction that my content can positively transform the souls listening to my lecture which is what really excites me.

That first semester Bible elective I taught at BFA had fifteen upperclassmen who were dealing with a whole lot of drama that term. I knew a snippet of the crushes and crushed dreams of high school relationships, but for the most part, I was out of the loop. I stayed in touch with one of the students from the class long after graduation. Years later, she talked me through the majority of the drama that linked the students with strained relationships and general mistrust before they started my class. She told me about how every student dropped the drama at the door when they walked into Spiritual Formation class everyday. I didn't see a lot of the friction between students because it disappeared in my classroom. Then, she told me about how they created a group chat when I was in the hospital.

Something beautiful happened every day in second period as these fifteen teenagers each recognised a sacred opportunity to learn, leaving behind petty popularity contests and prioritising their actual spiritual formation. I thrived in the environment where I was free to teach creatively. There was no actual curriculum for the class, so each unit I'd tell the prescribed topic to the students, and they would vote on proposed activities and avenues to learn.

During my grad school class on educational theories, I remember being so excited to try different methods of instruction, and that Bible elective was a playground for me as a teacher. I tried out projects and papers, lectures and prayer walks. I moved around the classroom as much as possible. I made the students shove the desks out of the way so we could sit on the floor for story time while I read them *Haroun and the Sea of Stories* by Salman Rushdie and led discussions about how the text inspired each of us to understand and share our faith with others.

Rushdie's children's novel is one of my all-time favourite books, and it was easy for me to justify a week of class time to jolt my students out of their malaise before Christmas break. I'd asked my department chair if I could take the time to do this when apologetics wasn't strictly part of my class, but if we were talking about being spiritually formed, we should talk about articulating our spiritual ideas. Russ had no hesitation in letting me teach whatever I thought would spiritually form these kids and fit the course objectives, so I danced down the hall to tell my students.

When we made it to the scene with the battle between the silent and speaking armies, my students were primed to see the value in talking through the weaknesses of their beliefs before facing people who would attack them. I'd already explained how Rushdie wrote the story as a compilation of bath time stories to his son while he was in hiding from religious leaders who wanted to kill him for suggesting people evaluate the weaknesses in his own religion. To this day, it was one of my most exciting moments as a teacher. I saw my students struggling to engage with spiritual disciplines, and I found a creative way to help them connect the dots between what they claimed to believe as Christians and how they expressed that to other people. We then soared into their final project which was choosing a couple of spiritual disciplines and practicing them for several weeks before writing a reflection paper on the experience.

I was moved to tears by multiple papers as I read how students were transformed by engaging in their faith in new and creative ways.

Not every student had a radical, life changing experience in that class, and not all of the ones who claimed to have discovered great insights had that stick long term in their life. As a teacher, I can't always know the impact I'm going to have on the lives of my students. This is where I agree with the science that says my passion has to be rooted in my content. I know my content has the power to transform lives; I just don't know which lives will be changed. So here I add my theory that, because I can't know which students I'll impact, I have to believe that each unique person made in the image of God who sits through my lessons has the potential to be radically transformed by the activity I facilitate or lecture I lead.

No matter the reputation a student brings into my classroom, I love them all immediately. Some of them are easier to keep loving throughout the semester, and some of them love me in return. Regardless of their feelings towards me, I consider it a sacred duty to help students see that my content is interesting and relevant to them. I'm not always successful, but I improve every class I teach.

In some ways, I feel badly for that first group of students who had me as their teacher because there was so much I didn't know. In other ways, they are the lucky ones who had me fresh out of grad school and excited to try out every new thing and discovered great success with the innovation in my classroom. Several years into my teaching career, I inevitably found some routines that needed to be shaken up a little bit to see if I could be more effective with my next round of students.

During my high school years, I had a number of seasoned educators trained during the "sage on the stage" era of education that expected all lessons to be a lecture where the teacher was the expert disseminating information to students, but during my own training as an educator, I discovered the research backed the more innovative professionals using "guide on the side" methods that encouraged students to learn how to learn. There's a wide range of research about how this is better for our technology-oriented society which needs to have citizens adept at teaching themselves in order to advance all disciplines in the future.

My grad school professors were quick to support the combination of both strategies to discover what was most effective with each group of students. Quality educators are constantly evaluating their efficacy and looking for how they can be better teachers each year. Before I even got into the classroom as a teacher, I had already internalised the fact that I was going to always need to be a lifelong learner if I was ever going to be an effective educator. I would obviously know more about my content than my students, but if I wasn't modelling excitement about the limitless potential of my learning, I was going to be imposing limitations on their learning in my classroom.

The day that I think I know everything I need to teach is the day I'm ready to die.

All through college, my plan had been to get my teacher's license and return to teach at the high school where I graduated, but I, unfortunately, wasn't going to be able to do my student teaching experience at that school. My university had easily placed student teachers at schools across the greater Portland area, but somehow I became a difficult one to place. My supervising professor knew I wanted to teach at a Christian school, so they looked for a private school placement for me, but the only school that was able and willing to take me was in Vancouver — an hour and a half drive from my Beaverton apartment through the rush hour traffic on both ends of the commute. My other option was to drive the opposite direction out to the boonies to teach at Gaston Jr./Sr. High School.

Gaston is a tiny, one stoplight town that the hicks and bogans in Forest Grove refer to as "hick town." They actually play in the same sports league as the high school I attended, and I distinctly remembered when our basketball team defeated the Gaston team on their home turf during my senior year. Our school hallways were filled with retellings of the conquering Falcons going out to their bus to discover the tires had been slashed. That was my only impression of Gaston, and now I was being told it was essentially my only student teaching option. It was still going to be a forty-five minute commute one way, but I'd be able to take back roads and have a charming, woodsy drive.

Before the school officially agreed to the placement, I had to drive out there to meet the principal and the two English teachers who would be my cooperating teachers during my two semesters of teaching experience. In our program, we'd been given very specific instructions on professional attire, and we were told we always had to remember we represented our university and needed to dress accordingly. I wore a skirt I'd stolen out of my mom's closet the year before so I would look like a grown up, but I felt incredibly overdressed when I sat down at the round table with the Gaston crew. One of the teachers was wearing jeans and an Oscar the Grouch t-shirt.

Soon into the school year, I recognised that I was alienating myself from the student body when I showed up in high heels that click-clacked pretentiously across the linoleum while the rest of the staff showed up in clean and tidy outfits that frequently included jeans and t-shirts. One day, another teacher even showed up in pyjama pants, but that was an extreme. Generally, the weekday attire was a comfortable-casual that matched the students. I adjusted as much as I felt possible without breaking my university's dress code rules.

That was the first of many unspoken lessons Christina taught me during my time in her classroom. I noticed immediately that she was comfortable with students, and they were comfortable with her. I learned to avoid alienating myself from students in subtle ways. I've increased in my sensitivity in that area each year, but it was a critical first step to adjust my footwear. I'd also noticed from observing Christina and my other co-operating teacher Maddy that while they had vastly different styles, both of them used proximity intentionally and to their advantage. I moved around the classroom a lot, and I found myself crouching to the level of students to give a body language indication that I wasn't looking down on their questions because I wasn't physically looking down on them at all. That was a particular strategy I had to adjust when I found myself teaching from a wheelchair, but I've remained sensitive to the response students have to my physical presence.

I also caught early on that Christina was highly effective with students after quickly building close rapport with them because instructions felt like requests rather than her being a demanding taskmaster. It was a personal style issue, and she talked to me about how it was effective for her, but that Maddy had success with a different style of engagement. After watching Maddy, I recognised that she also had a solid rapport with her students, but she elicited the response after establishing a culture of no cut corners. Clearly, both of these quality educators loved their students and found ways to connect and teach according to their own personalities. At the start of the school year, Christina encouraged me to try out different styles and figure out what I was most comfortable with. I could see that both Maddy and Christina loved their students, and I could see that the students knew that and were willing to open up to them at different points in class.

Even though I was only going to be the student teacher in the room for half the year, I really loved the students at Gaston. I think one or two of them might have even liked me too. I struggled a lot in connecting with those students, and my classroom management had a rocky start because of it. I found my footing near the end of the first semester which was just in time to leave that freshman English class for the next term when I was teaching the sophomores.

There were small glimmers of real human connection and learning that happened in that freshman English class though. One day in particular stands out as I was wandering around the room helping students to outline the essay that only six out of forty-five students would end up completing for me. A table group of girls was stuck on deciding what they wanted to write about, and there was a rare moment where this group that could only be described as Gaston's version of *Mean Girls'* "plastics" saw my humanity and were shook to their core.

"Why do we have to write these stupid essays?"

"It's not just because I'm mean; I promise. Writing is a really helpful life skill for whatever career you want. You'll always need to be able to articulate yourself to others. Remember when we talked about that with the journal prompt from a few weeks ago? Being able to describe your thoughts and feelings well is helpful in any job if you want to be successful."

"Like, to get a good paying job?"

"Yeah, any job that you have, especially ones that you want to get promoted in. It will help if you've developed the ability to express yourself well."

"How much do you get paid for this job?"

"Oh, I don't get paid to do this."

"*What?*"

"Well, I'm just a student teacher, so I'm learning to be a teacher. Obviously, the other teachers get paid, but I'm paying my university to train me to teach."

"Wait, so you're *paying* to teach *us?*"

"Yeah."

"That's crazy."

"Well, I do want to be a teacher who gets paid, but I have to learn to do it first."

"But, this is a terrible job. I can't believe you would do it without getting paid, and you're actually *paying* to do it."

"I really love teaching, and I love the chance to help students learn. I want to do it well, so it's worth paying to learn from good teachers."

There was a newfound respect from the aspiring cheerleader who, in a dramatic show of defiance a couple of weeks before, had ripped up a detention I wrote her. Another one of the girls started to watch me a lot more closely for the remainder of my time in the classroom. She'd been shuffled around several schools across a couple districts in western Oregon, and her home life was pretty rough. She showed up in the middle of the quarter with a reputation for being a difficult student along with warnings from the principal that she might not last at our school if her record was any indication of her expected behaviour.

Young and naive, I was nervous about what this loose cannon was going to do in my already overwhelming period of angsty freshman. In fact, she turned out to be delightful in my class, and when she first saw the crack in the "teacher" persona, she looked for more opportunities to learn about who I was as a person.

"Hey, Ms. Hewett," she found herself the first student in my class one day.

"Hey, you're early," I responded as I finished typing out some notes for the lesson and pulling up attendance.

"Yeah, I actually like this class."

I'd seen her in history class during one of my observations; I knew she wasn't lying.

"Hey, I was wondering about that tattoo on your foot. I've seen it a couple times."

I looked down at the outside of my right foot which was facing her. I was wearing a pair of my roommate's ballet flats that were loose and slipped off my heel when I sat down in tall chairs. "Uh-huh," I waited to hear what exactly she was going to ask. Legally, she was opening a door for me to answer fully and honestly, but I needed to know how interested she was. In American public schools, teachers are forbidden to proselytise or bring up their own religious convictions, but they can answer any student-initiated questions about personal faith and beliefs.

The Greek word *doulos* is permanently etched on my foot. I'd only had the tattoo for a couple months at this point, but I'd wanted the mark for six years before I committed the ink to my skin. *Doulos* means "slave" in Greek. Bondslave in particular, so it means a slave who had willingly committed their life to the master. I learned the word when I was studying the book of James as a senior in high school. The first verse opens with "James, a *doulos* of Christ," and I learned that a lot of the apostles took the term as a descriptor of their relationship with Jesus.

"What does it mean?" My student brought me back to the present.

"Well," I began cautiously, "It's the Greek word for bondslave... In ancient Roman culture, they had a kind of slavery where people go free after a period of time, but if the slave decided that the master took good care of them, they could choose to be permanently marked and stay a slave in that home forever. I chose to be marked because I believe there is someone worth being committed to for life who can take better care of me than I can do all on my own."

I paused, wondering if I was making sense to this anti-authority rebellious teenager who had likely never been to church. She nodded slowly, thinking about my words.

"I get that," she said, "I understand wanting to do that. I think I could want to do that too."

Another student came into the room and ended the conversation, but I could tell that girl was still watching me closely the rest of the year. I don't know how much she remembers about *To Kill a Mockingbird* from reading it in my class (though she seemed really excited about her map of Maycomb), but I think I taught her something that mattered.

When I think back on my years as a student, very few lessons stand out. Instead, I remember the patterns with which my teachers engaged me. I remember that they cared about me as a person, and as an afterthought to me growing as a person, they were also excited when I got good grades. I remember more details of Mr. Weber's stories about his college pranks than the details of his Old Testament lectures. However, he's the teacher who made me research James which first started my fascination with living out my faith in a way that included a permanent mark to remind me and declare to others my commitment to Jesus. I remember him storing snack food in his desk for me and letting me hide in his room during lunch when I was at the height of my anxiety attacks triggered by a number of my peers. I remember him encouraging me to pursue a Bible degree in addition to the English major because it was going to help me be a better follower of Jesus. I remember him teaching me.

I try to create a similar learning environment that allows students to recognise my teaching as more than just a lecture. Sometimes it stands out in a particular lesson when eager learners teach their peers through project presentations.

"Yes, as my group members have shared, there are lots of details within creation that point to the existence of a God which is what the teleological argument for the existence of God is about. But the most important reason we have is pigeons. Pigeons are legit."

There was a pause for laughter at this point. I had been chuckling through Bryce's contribution to the presentation and laughed loudly at this point.

"They have all these super special developed things about them, and it's just impossible to think that there wasn't a God who wanted to make these awesome birds."

He rambled quite a bit more, but the gist was, "Pigeons are legit; ergo, God exists."

I was full on laughing through the last bit of his explanation, but he got the point across that the teleological argument for the existence of God is based on the details of creation that point to a loving creator.

It was near the end of the school year, and I let the students do their apologetics activities based on their interest. This particular group had wanted to investigate some of the arguments for the existence of God. I'm always clear to tell the students that none of these are proofs that God exists but rather that they give us rational explanations which support our faith in the existence of the God of the Bible. This particular student had been excited to read in his research that proponents of this position could look at the intricate details of how pigeons could forage and thrive and see it as a reflection of a loving God who cared for the birds of the air, the fish of the sea, and the ridiculous teenagers in my classroom.

I've found students learn better when they laugh. I learn better that way too. I look for the joy, the humour, and the fart jokes in class because if I can connect the content to the laughter, it's more likely to stick in the students' memories. I love the spontaneous moments that will help the students to see the relevance of the class's content. They might not find the immediate relevance with the laughter, but the longer I can stick it in their brains, the more likely they will have opportunities to see the significance of the lesson. When I was revising the final exam for this class period, I snuck in an addition to the multiple-choice question about the teleological argument. I asked which argument for the existence of God used things like "legit pigeons and the perfect distance from the sun to the earth" as evidences of a loving God. As I proctored the exam,

I watched students turn the pages and thoughtfully fill in the scantron bubbles to show they remembered and understood the four steps of Bible study and the basics of Calvinism compared to Arminianism. I kept my eyes on Bryce when he flipped to the second to last page. I had already seen a couple other students look up at me and point to the exam with a wry smile when they reached question 87. Bryce broke into a full grin as he looked up at me.

Pigeons might not be a relevant part of my students' daily lives, but a different student from this particular class period sent me a picture of herself surrounded by pigeons in the streets of Rome during her senior trip the next fall. I don't care if they remember the word "teleological" when they see pigeons, but if they remember that pigeons are legit, they will remember there's a logical reason to believe in a loving creator God. Ideally, they'll connect that to the God of the Bible and look for how they can use the steps of Bible study they learned in my class to foster loving relationships with God and other people.

Knowing that those laughter-filled lessons are the exception, I have to hope that I can integrate the content learning with those unique, funny moments that will stick in their memories long after they leave my class.

Years after I taught her Bible elective during my first semester in Germany, I had a student tell me she still remembered the day that I got so excited that I ripped my boot off, threw it across the room, peeled off my sock, tossed it the opposite direction. The image stuck, along with the message that the Bible might change their life enough someday to permanently mark something on their body like the exposed *doulos* tattoo on my foot. Remembering how that visual worked, I brought several pairs of shoes to display through my chapel talk two years after my accident and the climax of my brief testimony was pulling off my right shoe to show off the tattoo again. Another year and a half later, a senior who was about to graduate told me how moved she was by that chapel talk and how she had cried during my testimony.

Every teacher would love it if their students listened with rapt attention to every lecture and could recall the laboured-over details of lessons, but my teaching career taught me that my greatest teaching moments happen outside the classroom. Students are listening all the time, and I'm constantly surprised at what sticks. It's a delicate combination of in and out of class material that they retain and take with them, so I always have to be aware of what I'm saying during any given interaction. Lessons don't end when the bell rings. In fact, the best lessons happen when the students perk up after the bell.

Bryce gave his "pigeons are legit" lesson late in the semester, but he'd chosen to learn much earlier in the semester during an after-class lesson I didn't mean to teach. He was a boisterous student who sat himself in the back row next to his best friend and soon to be girlfriend and signed his name as "your favourite student ever" the first week I met him. He's not the first student to try to claim that title, but I had no basis to know how much I'd actually like this kid. I had a sense he genuinely wanted to learn about the Bible in my class, but he was also a really chatty and distractible student.

"Bryce, hold up for a sec," I asked him as the bell rang during the second week of class. I wanted to find out for sure if he was interested in learning from me or if he was just a goof-off. I had another student who I was helping with the in-class assignment, so I wrapped up the conversation with her before I could give Bryce my full attention.

That brief interaction had given two of Bryce's senior dorm brothers time to come into the room and flank me before I had a chance to talk to him. They were known to frequently hang out in my room after school to talk about theology or to come to my house to bake cookies and discuss how to live more like Jesus.

"Yes, ma'am?" Bryce looked nervous, much more nervous than I intended him to be. It was only made worse by the two tall young men standing on either side of me waiting to discuss the nuances of what it meant to be a Christian advocating for the oppressed in today's nuanced American political landscape.

"Look, I just want to know if you're interested in actually learning in this class."

"Say yes," one of the seniors demanded without giving Bryce a chance to speak for himself.

"Dude, let him answer for himself," I said.

"Yes, ma'am, I do."

"Okay, then I'm going to help you learn."

"Do whatever she tells you," the other senior insisted.

"That's all; I just needed to know. You can go."

Bryce bolted from the room.

"Guys, you weren't supposed to intimidate him. I just wanted to find out if he was interested in being pushed to grow in my class."

"He should be."

"You can't make that decision for him."

The next day in class, I greeted students as they came in and watched Bryce pull his best friend to the front row.

"Dude, why are we sitting here? I don't want to."

"No, man, we have to."

I wasn't meant to overhear the comments, but I couldn't keep the smile off my face. Bryce didn't stay in the front row, but he did keep learning through the rest of the year. He stayed in my room to talk with other students about how to live out his faith, and he came to make cookies at my house and ask me about controversial theological issues with his dorm brothers.

Bryce died two years after I first drafted this memoir. He had opportunity to read and give his consent and approval for me to include this chapter before he passed. When Bryce passed, I actually published the excerpt about him on my blog as part of my grieving process.

I wrote this addition in the first year after leaving the classroom as an educator. One of my favourite coworkers graciously said I was still an educator as I transitioned from being a classroom teacher to a youth pastor. My life still involves teaching young people theology, and I still have no idea which moments will stick and what insights I share will matter to young people or even my team of volunteers who I lead and coach.

As I think about the twists and turns the lives of my former students have taken, I recognise that I can only plant or water seeds and guess at their end point based on their trajectories. When someone is just a hair off of true north, they will end up miles away from their destination if they don't recalibrate. As I began one of my last years in the classroom, a student returned to see me the first week of school and proudly put a framed piece of art on my desk. It was a simple print of the quote, "The best teachers are those who show you where to look but don't tell you what to see."

Every teacher knows they won't reach every student, but I do hope that I'll continue to show people around me where to look and watch their eyes light up as they see something new.

9

On Learning

Good educators are lifelong learners. I want to model that for my students, and hopefully all of my peers do as well. Certainly, some are better at this than others, but as long as we are all moving in the direction of new learning, we can inspire higher learning from our students.

I've wanted to be a teacher off and on since I was in first grade because of how much I loved learning and how exciting Mrs. Sprecker made it. She was one of many fabulous teachers who excited me about new content. Plus, I was really good at regurgitating answers all the way through high school. It was in high school that I decided I did want a career as a teacher and that my passion was English literature because I realised there was always more to find in a book. There was no answer key for an essay. This sunk in over time through key experiences in Mrs. Maki's English class.

I remember the sharp discovery of her differentiation process, comparing her comments between students when I was in tenth grade. My best friend was home sick from school for a couple days, and I was collecting homework to bring him. Mrs. Maki handed over his corrected *Highwayman* essay and warned me that his grade reflected the effort and improvement he'd made — just as mine did. He got an A- while I had a B+. I was livid when I read through his retelling riddled with grammatical errors and lacking in imagination. Then I realised that Mrs. Maki had been pushing me to a higher standard every year in her class. If she was doing the same for Kenny, he just had much further to go in his writing. Mrs. Maki wanted me to always excel in my strengths, so she needed to challenge me in my writing.

While I was still kind of miffed about getting a lower grade for better work, I was inspired to always improve my essays after that. Grades in my class are always linked to the same rubric for each student, but I often have students that I challenge in their personal growth to be better learners. When we rolled out a new grading policy school wide, I had a lengthy conversation with a student in my class about how to excel in learning. This particular student was looking for a reason not to manipulate the system to his advantage.

"I need a good GPA to get into schools, and if I just do the minimum work on certain assignments, I can guarantee the lowest grades will be erased and only put the effort into key assessments. How is that encouraging learning?"

Ever the theologian alongside educator, I turned to how the student saw himself as a follower of Jesus.

"It shouldn't matter what your grade is if you care about representing Jesus in how you behave in class."

I could proof text it with Colossians 3:23: whatever you do, whether your homework or lunch time conversations or dorm chores, do it all as if working for the Lord and not for people. I might have even brought that verse up at some point in that conversation, but I don't really remember. I remember desperately wanting this student to connect the patterns of behaviour that he had in his schoolwork to the fact that he called himself a Christian. When I prepare my lesson plans, I happen to be teaching theology, but I think about the details of how I'm presenting material in a way that honours God.

I think this mentality was ingrained in me through the pattern of learning that formed me during my years at Multnomah University in Portland.

"You should totally come visit us at Multnomah," Sarah told me when I was still a high school senior. She then turned to Rachel, "Don't you think Laura would love Miss Pothen? She's got to come visit our British literature class if she wants to be an English teacher."

"Yeah, and she should come to my psychology class too. But definitely Miss Pothen will be her favourite."

"Oh, and she has to visit Ray's class! Laura, you're going to love these professors."

I was still unsure where I was going to university, and Sarah and Rachel were two of the coolest university kids I knew. Seventeen-year-old me had been happily trailing after them in service and participation at our fledgling church plant, and I was eager to spend more time with them. We looked at the calendar to see what day was best, and I had a long weekend off at my school while they still had university classes. I packed up my overnight bag and headed to the greatest sleepover of my life.

Sarah and Rachel checked me in at the front desk and walked me down the hall to a room which, unbeknownst to all of us, was not too far from where I would live just two years later. After hours of laughing while watching pirated DVDs of *Boy Meets World* and flipping through bridal magazines where Sarah picked out the wedding designs for each of us, we finally went to sleep. (I kept the full-page dress advertisement selected for me and came across it over ten years later remembering how far I'd come as a person with the help of friends like Sarah and Rachel.)

Both of them were in Ray Lubeck's History and Poetry class, and I was completely captivated by this wise, moustached man who clearly knew the book of Job inside and out. Literally the next day, I would be visiting an Old Testament survey course at Concordia University, and after Ray's lecture, I dominated over all the Concordia students on their exam review period. Like, the professor actually shamed his students at the end of the activity because the high school students visiting for a university preview weekend who were supposed to be a joke team handily won mostly due to my learning in Ray's one lecture. I realised then the superior education Multnomah offered when it came to not only biblical studies but other courses as well; however, it still took me a full year at Concordia before I actually transferred to the better learning environment. I thought frequently of the preview I had of Ray's class and was eager to sign up for his Bible Study Methods course my first year as a student there. My awe of how exciting he made ancient Hebrew poetry was renewed every lesson in his classes.

Perhaps even more memorable during my visit at Multnomah was the chance to sit in a literature class. The British Literature course was in the library basement, and we showed up early to rearrange the desks in a circle. I felt awkwardly exposed to all the mature, intelligent, older students as a young high school senior, so I kept as quiet as possible, eager to absorb all the knowledge possible from my friends and their peers. Rachel and Sarah gave me a brief synopsis of the passage of *Paradise Lost* that we would be discussing, and I was excited to see what a university literature class was like as the rest of the students pulled out their annotated copies of the text and prepared to take notes on the imminent discussion. Not a second before the clock said the class should start, a tall, thin Indian woman strode into the classroom and instructed the students to stand for prayer. The energy of a room changes when Domani Pothen enters because she brings an extra dose of the Holy Spirit everywhere she goes. A friend of mine once said, "Miss Pothen knows when Jesus is coming back; she just isn't telling us." Dr. Pothen would be horrified with the comment, but it sums up well her relationship with Jesus and with students.

She is loved and feared across campus, and in her classroom, students are eager to impress her while simultaneously terrified of disappointing her. She's always twenty steps ahead of the conversation in any given class period, and my preview day was no exception. I could see in her eyes the excitement about the connection she was making between Milton's text and the theological implications in her students' lives, but not all of the class had caught up with the point she was trying to make. Certainly I didn't fully get it, but I had tracked with the majority of the argument she was making, so when she asked the silent room, "Are you with me?" I involuntarily nodded in agreement. "*See!*" She pointed at me and leaned forward, capitalising on the trance with which I listened to her, "Even our guest gets it, and she hasn't read all of today's text! It's so clearly here in what we've presented."

Part of me wanted to shrink and disappear with the attention I'd inadvertently drawn to myself, but the rest of me was completely captivated by the magnificent ideas presented in the hour visit I'd had in the class.

"So what did you think?" Rachel asked me after we reemerged from the library basement to the bright spring sunlight.

"I want to learn everything I can from that woman. She's so smart! I've never seen anyone other than my high school English teacher who can already see the next three comments in a conversation, and that woman was like a dozen steps ahead of everyone in the room."

"Yeah, she's brilliant."

When I finally did transfer to Multnomah, I took nearly every class Dr. Pothen taught, even multiple ones that weren't required for my degree just because I knew she would help me to learn more. In fact, during my time there, the required ENG 304 Advanced Writing course was done away with in favour of a significantly lower level ENG 220 Critical Reading and Writing. I'd already taken the higher level, and had no requirement to take a 200 level course my senior year, but with Dr. Pothen's permission, I signed up for it anyways.

"I'm so devastated for all the students who will never get the joy of taking Advanced Writing," my friend Desiree lamented when the change was announced. "I bet it's all those whiny pastoral majors complaining that Dr. Pothen makes them do too much work." She was probably right; pastoral majors are notoriously whiny.

"But now she's teaching a new class, and I wanted to be able to say I took every class that she taught when I graduated."

"I'm sure you could probably take this class."

"Do you think it would be worth it?"

I went ahead and asked her directly what value she thought there would be in me taking ENG 220 after already having the Advanced Writing learning. This is the same woman who once publicly chided a student who had the audacity to say they didn't learn anything from a particular chapel speaker. "What arrogance do you have to have to think you can't learn something from every other person made in the image of God? And if this person has gone through the process of getting the opportunity to speak in chapel, even if it's not the greatest message, there is always *something* that the Holy Spirit can speak to you. It is your responsibility to listen for that." She was much more gracious in her explanation to me that I would still be able to learn from her in ENG 220.

That class was a breeze academically on one level because I already had achieved the objectives the rest of the class were working towards. Knowing I had the foundation of those academic objectives already, Dr. Pothen was able to challenge me to step up to a new level of reading and writing beyond the course objectives. She met me where I was at, and she drew out my excitement when she asked me what insight I found in Adrienne Rich's essay "When We Dead Awaken: Writing as Re-Vision."

"Well, the first time I read this essay in Advanced Writing, I hadn't read any Ibsen or Woolf, so I didn't catch all the allusions. This essay is littered with parallels to *A Room of One's Own*. I have no idea what I've been missing in loads of other works now, but in this one, I'm so glad I had the chance to go back and see with deeper insight what she was connecting to. Now, her comments about having space to write and reimagine resonate so much more because I know about Woolf's struggle and cry for women to have the privilege to write."

"Yes! You're getting at what Adler and Van Doren reference in the textbook; those layers of reading are only possible when you return having read more interlocutors."

We had to have that conversation over again when I was too overwhelmed by my inadequate understanding of *Beowulf* to write my essay by the due date.

"I just know I'd write such a better essay if I had another week to just read the text a dozen more times. It's so rich, and I'm only scratching the surface of understanding it."

"Yes, but the due date is Friday, so write the essay based on this level of reading, and you can come back to the text later."

It wasn't my greatest writing, but it was sufficient for the learning objectives of the course to get me high marks. And Dr. Pothen knew I would keep learning the content long after I'd submitted the essay. My thesis was related to the efficacy of kinship ties and peace-weavers when they are voluntary rather than forced. I'm still working out my loyalties and their impact based on earned admiration or expectations of alliance. One thing is for sure, I'm devoted to Dr. Pothen and her consistency in pushing me to pursue Jesus in every aspect of my life. She knew urging me to be a better reader and writer would make me a better Jesus follower, and I'm so grateful for her influence.

During my final years at Multnomah, I was privileged to be one of her writing tutors who helped her 100 and 200 level English students improve their essays as well as work with any other motivated students who wanted English nerds to go over their work. The role was a coveted position among students because writing tutors had weekly meetings with Dr. Pothen where we discussed the texts she was teaching in addition to others we read together. The tutor meetings were a highlight of my week because I could learn from my peers about how they were engaging with texts differently than I did while also seeing how Dr. Pothen could weave our insights together into a higher thought that helped us to leave the meeting more in love with Jesus. Please forgive the poetic nostalgia; those meetings were genuinely insightful and delightful.

I began my career as a writing tutor very, very intimidated by the rest of the team, but I ended my term as confident because it was the role of the perpetual learner who encouraged learning in others. I wasn't teaching the texts, but I was partnering with the student as we looked for how to bring out insight in their essays, and I got to learn new things from every creative thesis that came to me. I also learned that some pastoral majors are major whiny-pants. (The stereotype was a running joke with the English majors, but the arrogant students who didn't want to waste their time at Bible college on a literature class came from several different majors.) My time as a learner under Dr. Pothen shaped me into the teacher I would become who presents content as a co-learner. Clearly, I know my content when I teach high school students, but I get excited every time I teach a lesson on the mystery of the Trinity because I'm that much closer to understanding how the divine dance works between these members. I speak with stronger conviction about the character of Jesus each semester because I know him that much better, and when I get to the lesson on the Holy Spirit, I would tell the students that if I seem to have an off day teaching, they can ask me if I forgot to pray for the Holy Spirit to fill me up that morning. I want my students to see me eager to learn because there is that much more to learn about the discipline. Dr. Pothen modelled that for me because she was genuinely excited to hear new insights from students while also having prepared deep wisdom to share with us.

On one of my return visits to America, I listened to Dr. Pothen give a sermon on how Jesus can redeem our wounds just as his wounds are redeemed. Afterwards, she sat next to me, and we reflected on the powerful work of redemption playing out in my own wounds, and she was just as excited about the layer of depth I could add to the message as I was about hearing the healing words of truth. We both learned from each other in that interaction, and that's the kind of relationship I hope to inspire with my own students.

As I grew as an educator, I had the privilege of adapting Ray Lubeck's curriculum for university students to a high school level and teaching the basics of exegesis and hermeneutics through Ray's words in *Read the Bible for a Change*. I began telling students that if there was one thing they remembered from my class, I wanted it to be "the purpose of reading the Bible is to foster loving relationships with God and other people." That line comes verbatim from the first page of Ray's book, but it's a paraphrase of the words of Jesus who taught people to love the Lord your God with all your heart, soul, mind and strength and to love your neighbour as yourself. He taught us to love God and love others. The Bible, as a whole, tells us to foster those loving relationships with God and others. It's a big deal, and I wanted my students to learn that concept not only to regurgitate it but also to inhabit the meaning.

A career highlight for me at BFA was when I found myself with a microphone in a whole school assembly where I started the sentence, "The purpose of reading the Bible is —" only to be cut off by a solid third of the student body who had already taken my class literally shouting, "*to foster loving relationships with God and other people!*" Learning that sentence was a catalyst for a lot of young people who took my class to start reading the Bible purposefully and intentionally. Some of them also found the phrase a catalyst to change their habits as they engaged with others in the world around them. Within the first year of teaching that textbook, I discovered students were reminding themselves of the phrase and keeping it at the forefront of conversations about faith and life. One kid took it a step further as she realised she wanted to inhabit that concept and live each day with the reminder present in her life.

Lissy was a bit cautious, strangely nervous, even when she presented her idea to me.

"I want to get that tattooed on my arm," she said timidly.

I thought this was a great idea and told her so.

"I was thinking I'd get it in the handwriting of different people who've been significant in my spiritual journey," she went on.

"That's so cool!"

"Would you want to be one of the people?"

"I would be *honoured!*"

It took Lissy a few months to work up the courage to ask each person she cared about if they'd be willing to contribute a word in permanent ink on her arm. She came back to me and asked if I'd help her make the appointment to get it done. This was her first tattoo, and she had no idea where to go, so I gave her the contact information for the guy I went to in Schlingen for my previous two. It wasn't an easy bus route for me, but she asked if I'd come along. We ended up figuring out a car ride to and from the place, and I got to sit with Lissy while she lay on the tattoo bed watching Benny drag the sterile needle across her skin.

Once we finished, she carefully pulled her sweater back on over the bandaged skin before she returned home.

Over my last few summers in Kandern, Lissy would stretch out on my picnic table and soak up the warmth after dragging the umbrella to the perfect position to prevent sunburn during the extended conversations we'd have together. For a few weeks after her graduation, she actually lived with me, sleeping on my couch, sharing life on life, and learning how I lived out these Jesus things I learned while reading the Bible.

I can't count how many cups of coffee I drank while Lissy sat beside me with her cup of tea at my table and we opened the Bible together. We spent a season reading 1 Corinthians over and over again. Another time, we took a week to dig into the details of 1 Timothy. Other students and alumni would rotate through the space, but Lissy came consistently to practice reading and living out the lessons we found in the Bible.

In the years ahead, Lissy will continue to find new tables to lay across and new people to have tea with while discussing theology. I can't guarantee that Lissy will align with me on everything theologically, but we've actually talked a lot about the learning process I've had as a mentor and a Jesus follower, as one who disciples others and points people to Jesus. I'm not afraid of where Lissy will end up primarily because it's not my responsibility to shoulder her choices. But secondarily, I have watched her add other people who are committed Jesus followers into her life to learn from. She has at least five people she can have a cup of tea with; plus, she'll still call me somewhat regularly. She definitely sends me memes consistently.

When students would leave the tight knit community in Kandern where people understood their third culture context, my biggest encouragement was for them to find a community of Jesus followers who would love them and support them in their new location. I felt strongly about being a bridge to them from their BFA experience to wherever they went next, and I often kept in touch with young people. Over the years, I noticed a pattern that students who chose to stay isolated and disconnected from Jesus followers were more likely to drift away from any kind of commitment to Jesus they might have had. Conversely, those who plugged into a church or strong community seemed to deepen and grow in their faith.

Those who wanted to learn more about Jesus found the people who would teach them. When I look at Lissy, I see her seeking those around her who can help her to flourish. She hasn't got it all figured out yet, but a huge part of the learning process is knowing that there's a lifetime of things you have yet to learn.

10

On Graduation

I was somewhat underwhelmed by the idea of ceremony in anticipation of my hooding for my Masters in Teaching, but the program director emphasised the importance of the rite of passage a great deal in the weeks leading up to the graduation ceremony. At that point, I knew I was going to be moving to Germany in a few months' time, so I was already looking to what was next. Dr. Miller's reminders were significant in me slowing down to mark the moment of a changing season in my life. Although I was pretty cynical about the idea of ceremony leading up to that, I'm grateful Dr. Miller made me reconsider and take seriously that moment in my life.

I do believe that graduations are significant, but I don't believe we should spend so much time emphasising the ceremony and the single moments when the accomplishment is more important as part of a lifelong trajectory of learning and loving others. I love the celebration, but I don't love the pressure that comes along with it so often in American culture.

The whole concept is about marking a significant achievement, and I love the idea of having those "ebenezers" or obvious markers in life to look back on and see the moments in which we transitioned to another phase.

Having lived in three countries and taught students who've learned in dozens more, I've discovered that different school systems mark different years as landmark moments in the educational career of a learner. In my passport country, the transition from high school to college or university is by far the most significant, but there was also a big to-do at my school as students left junior high and entered high school. The school actually had to fight the formality as the students spent more and more money on fancy clothes, hair styles, and who knows what else surrounding the evening ceremony.

My eighth grade graduation lined up with my sister's high school graduation, and I remember realising the exponentially greater significance of that rite of passage, so I naturally spent the four years of high school stressing out about it. Okay, that's hyperbole, but I did see the culturally assigned significance of the moment.

When I moved to New Zealand, I learned the leavers ceremony here is a much different deal. There's still some pomp and circumstance, but I'm pretty sure they don't play "Pomp and Circumstance" at any of the events surrounding the leaving of school like we do in America. Students move somewhat uneventfully into Christmas break (the summer holidays down under) and then pick up at university in the new year. There're some small parties and general excitement about the end of the school year, but I saw none of the pressure and stress I've come to associate with the leaving of high school in America or even my international school in Germany.

In my experience, the entrance to elementary school is a bigger marker in the German culture. Students have a big cone filled with candy they bring to the first day of first grade, and the older students have a special welcoming ceremony. I love the idea of the celebration being the beginning of something. In America, the end of high school is the "start of the rest of your life," but what have you been doing for the last eighteen years if not living? I'm not proposing that we have some "welcome to university" celebration instead, though, because I think the binge drinking culture in America is bad enough on higher education campuses.

However, I would propose that we look for the moments that we want to celebrate and be intentional with them. Before you chastise me saying this is what I just described American high school graduations as, here's how I'd like to change it: instead of that outdated hat and gown that looks awkward and usually smells bad, why don't we have smaller ceremonies where students are given affirmations for what they've accomplished in high school and are sent out to pursue more good things in their next phase of life. I feel idealistic proposing this, but isn't the whole concept of a graduation ceremony about idealism?

Maybe it's not.

Maybe graduation is about shoving kids through, turning out another batch who've at least passed the minimum requirements at least.

Going through grad school, I grew somewhat cynical about the educational system in America. The whole behemoth is a sinking Titanic. I actually wrote a paper about that in my Foundations of Education class. I believe the American school system ought to be burned to the ground, scrapped, and rebuilt from the ground up.

We need to teach students how to learn better, and then when we see that they have developed that critical skill, we should have a party for each kid. When they make it, they deserve a celebration of the scaffolding they now have which will help them to transition into the next phase of life, pursuing a trade or higher education or whatever they want.

Then again, maybe we should reform the system from within, and the graduation ceremony can maintain its link to history with those silly tassels and stuffy robes.

For all the back and forth I have about the concept, what I do want to emphasise is that milestones matter. Just before graduating with my master's degree, the director of my program gave a heartfelt plea to our cohort to make this graduation ceremony a significant marker in our lives as we moved into our careers as teachers. While I was already cynical about the system at that point, I did slow down a bit to cherish the life I had in the moment.

In fact, each of the graduation ceremonies I've participated in as a graduate, I can see the value in marking the movement to a different phase of life. Kindergarten ended the childhood innocence as I learned why my sister didn't want to go to school everyday: learning cursive handwriting is hard. The transition from eighth grade to ninth was marked with a formal ceremony at my school, and I also changed campuses for the first time. Leaving high school, I found a lot more fear surrounded the exit into the big, wide world which I hated at first until I transferred to the oasis of Multnomah. Both my undergraduate and graduate university degree ceremonies were underwhelming moments but still stand as important markers in my life.

High school graduation ceremonies at Faith Bible High School were, once upon a time, an incredibly personal coming of age moment for graduates while simultaneously being a huge bore for people who didn't know more than one graduate. They've changed a lot over the years, but in the era of my own graduation, each graduate was given the chance to share some public thank yous for two minutes.

Naturally, this was a huge moment with tons of build up, and I was a complete mess when given my two minutes to shine. I had practiced over and over, and I just fell apart and started crying because I was leaving the place I loved so much which had formed me as a person so significantly. I had worked out the list of people I was going to thank, and I broke down after, I think, the second name. Honestly, it's one of my greatest embarrassments, and I considered not including this humiliation in print, but it feels dishonest to withhold it.

ON GRADUATION

My own teenage years were glorious in so many ways. Sure, I was suicidal and severely depressed for a quarter of it, but I also was up in front of the school exuding confidence each week of my senior year as the worship team leader. I had one of the most coveted student leadership roles, and I'd been widely acknowledged as one of the most responsible students in the school. I had spent time as queen of the school (though I preferred the term "princess"), and I had battled back up to this pseudo-confidence after a major depression that attacked my self-image; I felt something like a champion by graduation.

Despite the lows, which had been pretty low, I was mostly scared to leave what I knew so well. My school was tiny. I was in a graduating class of forty students, and we were the largest class in the school. I was heading to what felt like a massive university when I left, and I was scared that I was going to be lost amongst all the heathen masses (I also wasn't going to be surrounded by Christian teachers and mostly professing Christian peers for the first time in my life). I wanted my graduation ceremony to be perfect because it was going to be the culmination of my fabulous four years of high school.

It wasn't perfect, because nothing in life is.

At some point in the ceremony, I was involved in leading a worship song, but I don't remember which one (or two or three) we picked. I just remember being super ticked that one of the other co-leaders had refused to practice and had not told the PowerPoint guy what order he was going to do the verse/chorus/bridge of the songs he was leading because he wanted to be "led by the Spirit" on stage.

As part of the ceremony, graduates all scattered throughout the mega church handing out roses to up to five people who were influential in their personal lives. Over a decade after my graduation, I had a conversation with my mentor about how Faith Bible graduations go down, and I mentioned something about giving her a rose at my ceremony.

"I wasn't at your high school graduation."
"Yes, you were. I gave you a rose, Jen."
"No, you didn't. I didn't know you until you were in college."
"That's not possible. I gave you and Tina both roses."
"You gave Tina one, I'm sure, because she knew you in high school, but we weren't in each others' lives until you had already graduated."
"That's just not possible. I gave you a rose."

For the record, I'm going to maintain that I gave Jen a rose, but there's actually a good chance it was a woman named Shauna who moved away shortly after that and dropped out of my memory for the next decade. While this graduation ceremony was an important moment in my life, it clearly didn't hold as much weight in my long-term memory as I anticipated it would.

There was also the whole valedictorian ordeal. I'd been one of several "valedictorians" in my eighth grade class (I put it in quotes because it was a shady system to determine who received this title, and who really cares in eighth grade?), and my sister was valedictorian for both junior high and high school. It was an unspoken expectation in my house that I would receive this award in high school, so I breathed a huge sigh of relief when I managed to score the title along with six other classmates (we were a class of overachievers).

Andy gave the valedictory address because the six other valedictorians unanimously voted to have him do it since he was actually the smartest (and none of us wanted to give a speech). I don't remember what he said, but I do remember that I actually respected Andy a lot. He was the best dude in our class; he loved Jesus the most.

At the point in the ceremony where they gave us all medallions, we had to stand in front of the audience and take off those silly hats for our parents to present the awards. I was so devastated when the presentation of my medal was only captured by a blurry photo of my terrible hair and my mom laughing as I told her she broke the medallion. She had broken it, and I thought that was funny too — it was more the hair I was worried about in that bad photo.

Later that night, I cried about the fact that I cried during my two minutes of sharing. I had timed it beautifully so that I could have a few jokes and some deep insights, thanking the people who'd poured into me as a young leader, but I choked out a couple sobs that threw off the whole rehearsed thing. I also cried later because my dad wouldn't let me go to the party all my friends were at because we were hosting a dozen family members who had flown in from out of state to see me.

These are all silly things I can laugh about now. I'm actually thankful there aren't more photos of the mess of that night. There are enough available to the stalkers on Facebook, but they aren't something I look at often. As far as I know, there's no one watching any video evidence of that embarrassing two minutes either, so thank God for that. I'm pretty sure I'm the only one who remembers I cried because I know about half my peers had some tears involved, but I can't name any other individual who did. I don't even remember a single word anyone else said.

I just remember that Andy wouldn't let me introduce him as "my betrothed" because his grandparents were going to be there, so I called him my "allergy buddy" instead as I passed the microphone to him. We were never in danger of getting married, but our moms did dream about it for years as we grew up because they were best friends. I totally embarrassed that poor kid every time we were in public; Andy's an absolute champ, and his wife Betsy is a lucky woman.

You see, there's some great beauty in that moment in time when Andy and I graduated from high school, but what matters more is that we both were on a trajectory to spend our lives loving Jesus and others better. Years later, when I was getting ready to move to Germany, Andy and I got together for coffee to catch up on college, grad school, and life. He was still pursuing Jesus wholeheartedly, and so was I. I love the knowledge that we have that same marker of launching out of high school into lives that honour God.

I don't want to erase the memory of my high school graduation, but I wish that I had realised it was just a marker of how far I'd come in anticipation of the good I was going on to do. When I reached graduation from my undergraduate program, I was ambivalent to the whole concept of graduations. I'd been so disillusioned by my high school graduation experience that I pretended the undergraduate ceremony didn't mean anything.

I can't tell you how absolutely delighted I was to discover that I had a significantly louder surround sound cheer than any of the youth ministry majors who had brought their whole youth group to celebrate with them. Not only had my youth kids come, but almost two dozen other people drove across town to cheer me on in my accomplishment.

I absolutely loved my years at Multnomah. I ended my time with the coveted role of writing tutor, and I was so much more safe and secure in my identity than I had been leaving high school. Multnomah was safe and significantly more formational than my high school, and yet Multnomah was ever eager to send me out to change the world. I had spent the majority of my high school years anticipating getting a teacher's license in order to return to that same school to teach English.

While that would have been an admirable career, Multnomah professors wanted me to be a world changer rather than to turn around and hoard my talents in a small community which I considered safe. Some of them were more vocal about that than others, and my mentors at church were explicit in telling me that my dreams were too myopic. They were sensitive to the root problem — I didn't want to grow. I wanted to return to what was safe. It wasn't going to be a launching experience for me to go back to my own high school. For other people, it's a laudable celebration of championing people in their hometown; for me, it was a symptom of a deeply rooted fear that I couldn't do anything bigger and wanted a manageable career where I knew I could look like a success with relative ease.

When my students approach graduation season now, I try to encourage them that they are given a chance to make memories in this season and be launched into something new and beautiful. I want them to know that the graduation experience itself isn't the end of the world, and that it's also worth remembering — so they shouldn't get blackout drunk and forget the whole night. Some of them listen to my advice. Regardless of their attitude towards the graduation season, I've seen so many of them go on to thrive and a decent number go on to crash and burn post graduation. It's a different season either way.

I graduated from high school in 2007, and the first class of freshman that I taught when I arrived at BFA were slated to graduate in 2017, exactly ten years after my own high school graduation. I had a special bond with those kids, and when I broke my back and lost the opportunity to end the year as their English teacher, I was pretty devastated. It was an incredibly healing experience to get to teach thirty-six of the original forty-five in that class when they were juniors, and I found a significant number of new students who joined that year who were quite special to me. When they graduated in 2017, I drafted out a letter to them telling them how proud I was, and it was something I'd always planned to include in my memoir.

Then I accidentally wiped my hard drive that Christmas.

Then I met the class of 2018, and they won my hearts.

There were so many students that I taught as juniors in the 2016-2017 school year who were excited to learn in my class and had no image of me as anything other than the quirky teacher in a wheelchair. The seniors above them were the last students left at BFA who had known me as the quirky teacher who danced around the classroom before spending half a year in the hospital and coming back in a wheelchair.

I loved teaching juniors because I got to bond with them while teaching them and have a whole extra year to be around them before they left high school. I finally accepted student Facebook friend requests at graduation if they decided they wanted to keep in touch. The class of 2017 had tons of students who spent hours at my house after school baking cookies or talking theology while drinking tea. It was actually students in that class who had made tea time at my house an official thing. Tea and *pico de gallo*. Cookies came later. I thought it would die out with them, actually, but then the next round of juniors caught wind of the seniors spending time at my house all the time and asked to come along.

It came in small increments as one senior would bring his junior dorm brother along when none of his other senior friends were free. Another student asked if he could come along because he heard his girlfriend had been invited and wanted to continue conversations from class. Two new dorm students realised they had discovered a hangout option that wasn't the dorm or school, so they asked to use my kitchen for baking adventures. Some students even found out I'd feed them dinner if they asked me to. By the end of 2017, there were kids coming over regularly, nearly every day after school, and only half of them were seniors.

When school started up again in the fall, there were a list of students asking to come over for tea. By the time June came around, this new class had won me over almost entirely. I was so sure that the class of 2017 would always be the most important class to me, and here I was deeply attached to this new group of students.

I have a personal rule that I don't accept Facebook friend requests from students until they graduate, and by the time graduation day came around in 2017, nearly a third of the students in the graduating class had already sent the request and were waiting for approval. One of them had arranged with me that I would accept her request at the start of the ceremony so she knew she'd been Facebook friends with me a good two hours before I accepted all the other requests after the recessional. Apparently, there was then an announcement on their class group page that I was now accepting friend requests and a significant number more added me through the rest of the week.

BFA graduations are extra special events because, unlike monocultural settings, these students are never likely to gather together in a large group again. If they manage to make their way back to Kandern, the staff turnover makes it difficult for there to be much of the same sense of belonging they may have felt during their school years. In anticipation of this being their last moment together, the school tries to make it a special event that celebrates each student's time at the school, and as they receive their diploma, they also hear short personalised affirmations collected by the staff along with a verse chosen specifically for them by a small group leader or close teacher. I write notes and thoughts about most students, but there are usually only a couple who have a strong connection to me. In 2017, it was a much higher number, and I even signed up to go to the dessert reception in the gym after the ceremony to say goodbye to the students.

I had been talked into going to the event by one of the students who I'd taught both as a freshman and a junior.

"I never sign up to go to those desserts. They always send an email and emphasise that you are only supposed to go if you have a special connection with the class."

"You *do* have a special connection with us though — you taught us."

"Yeah, but most of the teachers taught you at some point, and everyone loves your class, so it's going to be full." I was looking for an excuse not to go; I'd have to find help up to the gym and then be trapped in a room full of people until I could find someone to help me back down the stairs and run away home. The previous year, I'd parked my wheelchair by the open door to the patio and literally booked it home before the principal even finished his closing remarks at the end of the recessional.

"But you taught most of us *twice*," this student seemed to think it was important that I show up, so I agreed to come.

I found a friend who would help me up the stairs and let me hang out with her while making snarky comments in order to avoid thinking about how I'd never see 90% of these kids ever again. Several students brought their parents up to meet me, and while I was delighted to tell each of them how wonderful I thought their child was, I was actually quite overwhelmed by the fact so many students sought me out.

I was all the more convinced that with this group gone, I'd be back in the background and only impacting a couple kids a year. When the fall came around and this new group of seniors insisted on coming over to my house the first week of school, I was pleasantly surprised. When they kept filling in my weeks and bringing along juniors and eventually fighting with juniors because they ought to have seniority on cookie baking opportunities, I was a little confused. But this new senior class was doing their very best to make sure I knew they loved me more than the previous class.

During the 2018 graduation ceremony, I was sitting next to Esther who was staying at my house for the event. I still had my same rule about not accepting friend requests on Facebook until graduation day. However, I'd agreed to accept an HBR boy's friend request at the start of the ceremony, then his roommate at the moment he got his diploma, followed by the rest of the class' requests later in the day, long after the ceremony was over. Once the students sat down after the processional, I got a message from the first kid saying, "Ha, I can do this now."

I had told my students to say their goodbyes to me during the week of finals. I had lots of cookie making happening at my house, and they were all told that was the last time they'd see me because I wasn't going to stick around for the mob that happens on the patio after graduation, and I wouldn't be going to the dessert with their parents. Keeping to my word, when the principal was explaining the procedure of graduates saying goodbye outside the auditorium followed by the dessert in the gym, I was wheeling myself home as fast as possible. Apparently, by the time the principal was finished, my two new Facebook friends had found Esther and asked her where I was.

Unsatisfied with the goodbye I'd given them the day before, they both came to my house later in the afternoon and climbed through my open kitchen window to complain that I'd bolted from the graduation ceremony.

"I *told* you I wasn't going to stick around and get stuck in that mob."

They were the first of about a dozen kids who trickled through my window that evening. I became a stop for a group to have dinner, and I laughed with all of them as they refused to use my front door. It's really not that difficult to open, but then again, it's not that difficult to climb through my kitchen window either.

The next day, I had a couple more come through to say goodbye, and I reflected on how the graduation marker was going to change each of these students. I think often to Dr. Miller's comments about making graduations be a significant milestone, and I still find myself conflicted. I don't want to overemphasise the moment, but I do cherish the intentional interactions when students get a chance to recognise this is their last goodbye. Or at least last goodbye for a while.

Surely this was a fluke, though, and throughout their junior year, I was open with the class of 2019 that I'd be away for totalisation the following year. I didn't think it would be that hard to part ways with this group. I'd taught about half of them both their freshman year and their junior year, and I was quite fond of them, but they didn't seem to reciprocate nearly as much as the two years above them had. In fact, multiple students in that class admitted to me late in their junior year that they'd spent the majority of their freshman year convinced I hated them and that it had taken nearly a whole year to convince them otherwise.

When I showed up to visit for two weeks around the opening ceremonies at the start of their senior year to say one last goodbye, I found myself having a conversation with an emotional senior during her study hall the first week of school. I was shocked to discover my leaving would have such an impact on her.

"I know this is just part of BFA, but it's going to be hard this year, and I've lost another group of significant adults in my life like you."

She had tears in her eyes, and my own vision got blurry as I heard her identify me as someone significant in her life.

"It was supposed to be easy for me to leave this year. I never expected it to be this hard."

When I said goodbye to her before flying to New Zealand for the year, she adamantly told me, "See you at grad."

"You know I can't promise that."

Graduation day was still a significant moment in her life, even without me, but that day during her study hall was a milestone for me. I won't stop anyone from making a fuss about graduations, but I will try to make people put their attention on the individuals in the moment.

When It's October Again

This time last year I believed in miracles.

I get why Sarah did it, why she told her husband, "Sleep with Hagar," because she was tired. It's not because she was nearing one hundred and didn't believe God could do miracles.

No, it's because she saw God's miracles pass her by.

Sure she was saved from Pharaoh and rape and her husband didn't die, but don't you see, she gave up asking for a child and God promised something that was too much to hope in again. It was too exhausting to see the monthly blood and know no son was coming, to watch her womb go dry and with it her dreams.

Don't tell me to expect the extraordinary.

Don't awaken love before it's time, Song of Songs warns. What about when the Lord whispers secret hopes and tells you to anticipate good that never comes? That hasn't come. Sarah gave birth to a son.

My story isn't over yet.

Joseph's story is long, decades fly by in short chapters, but he lived each hour between the dreams of reward and his brothers bowing down — and many of those were in prison. Lord, I hope no one told him "all things happen for a reason" while he rotted in jail. I hope he never heard "this is part of God's plan" when he was falsely accused of rape. Sure,

Joseph knew God was faithful, and we think of him as faithful too, but I just have to wonder, was there ever a night during those long years of slavery that he wondered aloud, "It's October again?"

You said soon.

Those heroes of faith all got their reward, and I trust your character remains the same. See, I can say the right words, but are you hearing my heart? That even when I know you love me, I don't see it in my current pain. Last year you said a miracle was coming, but now it's October again.

This time last year I believed in miracles.

11

On Following

In general, I prefer the term "Jesus follower" over "Christian" because it's less loaded and is a better descriptor of what I actually do with my life. I have read the book of Acts and have a Bible college degree, so I know the term Christian was a reclaimed slur meaning "little Christs" first used at Antioch and all that jazz. I'm all for reclaiming slurs when it's contextually appropriate; that's not really an issue for me. Rather, modern western culture has a different connotation for Christian that isn't exactly a slur, but it comes with a lot of baggage that I don't want attached to my religion (I'm also willing to use the word "religion" a lot more readily than I used to be).

The Pacific Northwest is a wonderful place to grow up, and it's got a distinctly anti-traditional religious bent in the air as people tend towards the mystical or scientific but shy away from the structures of organised religion. Soaked in that culture, I found myself eager to be associated with the Jesus of the Scriptures but not the Christians of the Crusades. That came most sharply into view for me when I was in high school and met a group of brothers and sisters in Christ who had travelled from a church in Texas to help my church plant invite people to our new services. I heard one of the college aged team members was telling locals we were a Baptist church.

"We're not a Baptist church," I informed him.

"Yes you are," he responded with what I can only describe as Texan confidence.

"Um, actually, no, we're not, and you really shouldn't be telling people that. It's going to keep them from showing up at services."

"Except you *are* a Baptist church. It just isn't in the name like 'First Baptist' or anything. You are Baptist."

I didn't appreciate the condescension, but I was mostly angered by the way this guy was unknowingly chasing people away from our services despite the fact we had a lot of Baptist theological alignment. We were deliberately non-denominational because of the aversion to organised religion rampant in the Pacific Northwest. More people were likely to show up at a non-denominational service than a Baptist service even if the content was identical. I knew this because of a lifetime growing up in this environment. It was then I learned that in large swaths of the Bible Belt in America, you don't choose *to* go to church, you choose *which* church to go to. It's a whole different culture.

That eager Texan volunteer was still my brother in Christ, but I realised that we followed Jesus differently based on our upbringing and contexts. We'd had lots of things in common, and we shared a passion for introducing others to Jesus, but we looked and talked differently in our home settings. I had far more interactions of solidarity with members of the Texan teams than cultural clashes, but it did shape my understanding of the church deeply.

Years later when I was preparing to leave for Germany, my mentor, Jen, asked me what I was most excited about, and I honestly answered that I was most looking forward to seeing Jesus outside of my cultural context. I knew there were certainly things about my understanding and expression of Jesus that were cultural trappings rather than core to the character of my Savior. Some of my most treasured experiences in the past several years overseas have been seeing the central practices of church that I can participate in across the globe while seeing the cultural flavour that changes based on where I am.

The clearest example of following Jesus with different cultural lenses has been communion in different churches. Growing up, I went to a church that used tiny rectangle wafers and the plastic cups with a half a swallow of grape juice passed to the congregants every Sunday. My parents taught me that we did it to remember the sacrifice of Jesus, and I heard the same explanation at Westport when I started attending there in high school. During college, I learned all the fancy terms like "transubstantiation" and "consubstantiation" and weighed the arguments of Luther and Calvin in response to the Catholic tradition. I was also put in charge of buying the bread and juice for occasional Friday night services. I horrified my friend Mark when I packed up the extra bread to take home and feed myself for the weekend.

"Isn't that, like, holy now?"

"No, we don't believe in that. It's just bread, and I'm a poor college student. It's free food. I'm not going to throw it away."

To be fair, the high church liturgy requires the priest to eat all the blessed bread that's unused in the sacrament so there's no wasting of the body of Christ. I watch that at the Anglican church too, the elements being carefully measured for the least amount of leftover.

During my first time in New Zealand, I was asked to lead communion in one of the Sunday services. In my introduction, I read Paul's 1 Corinthians explanation of communion from The Message because it includes this nice bit at the end that says, "You must never let familiarity breed contempt." I then went on to say that one of the greatest gifts I've had of moving outside of my passport country is seeing the church through a different culture. It shook me out of the dangerous complacency with the story of the Gospel, but I also found great comfort in finding the same Jesus outside of my cultural lens. Familiarity on its own isn't bad, but I need a constant reminder that it's Jesus that is familiar, not my cultural lens.

I will follow this same Jesus into any new culture. In fact, I had a lot of explaining to do to the medical staff at the rehab hospital after my accident because they didn't understand why an American teacher would move across the globe to a country where she didn't speak the language to teach students at a special school where they could pay less money to attend if their parents are missionaries. "Because Jesus" is an honest response, but that only makes sense to people who have met Jesus too.

I follow that ancient carpenter who was crucified and conquered death, but it's a strange story on the surface. I have to make sure my lifestyle backs up that message of love when I interact with other people. Sadly, there have been a number of vocal people throughout history who claimed to be followers though their lives don't seem to back that up. Jesus said you know a tree by its fruit, so I hope there's some fruit in my life that backs up my claim to be a genuine Jesus follower.

This brings me back to my initial statement that I prefer the term "Jesus follower" over "Christian." As an English major, I know that languages are living things, so I can be comfortable choosing my self-description based on the current cultural connotation. "Jesus follower" is more broadly understood to be people who practice the ways of Jesus; in many modern Western countries, "Christian" more broadly references people who associate with a religion as part of a cultural identity rather than personal lifestyle.

It took me years to reach this comfort level with these terms though, and I remember my early wrestling with the connotations of "Christian" and the other identifying terms that came up in my teenage years. As a DC Talk fan raised in the 90s, a random movie outing with friends in high school put my "Christianese" vocabulary into sharp contrast with the world.

"Sorry, folks, we can't get the projector working, if you'll all exit the theater, we'll give you vouchers to come see the movie on another day," a bored cinema employee told the sparse group at a midday spring break movie showing.

Kenzie, Rachel, and I exited the theater as directed and paused in the lobby to discuss our options as relatively poor high school students. We weren't really the shopping kind of girls, and we didn't have any money even if we were. We were more inclined to coffee, but a little short on cash for an extra Starbucks stop that day. Another group of three high schoolers came up and started chatting with us about our disappointment at not being able to see Johnny Depp on the big screen that afternoon. I'm pretty sure this occurred during one of the five or six times I went to see some iteration of *Pirates of the Caribbean* in theaters. It was a weekday, but we had the day off from school.

"Do you guys go to Liberty or Glencoe?" the strangers asked us.

"Oh, we all go to Faith Bible High School."

"Um, so are you guys like Jesus freaks?" the well groomed guy in the group asked.

"No!" Rachel answered emphatically.

"What do you mean by 'Jesus freaks'?" I asked. I'd grown up conditioned to hear the term as a compliment thanks to DC Talk, but it was clearly asked with a tinge of fear in his voice.

"Like do you hate gay people or different religious groups?"

"Oh, no," I said, "We're not those kind of Jesus freaks."

Visibly put at ease, our conversation continued as we talked, most likely about how Kenzie's complete ensemble was purchased at Hot Topic over the course of several months. Shortly after, we amicably parted ways with our new friends who we would never see or talk to again (this was pre-Facebook and smart phones).

I wasn't sure what to make of the situation for a while after because I was conditioned to see "Jesus freak" as a compliment, and I was additionally conditioned to expect the evil heathens of the world to persecute me for my faith. In that interaction, the fear my new acquaintance had in response to hearing we went to a Christian school made me consider that the "persecutors" and the "persecuted" were not such simple categories as I'd been led to believe. There is real persecution of Christians, but I'm not inclined to believe the non-existent "War on Christmas" counts. Instead, I've seen more and more of the stories like the scared teenager I met who have been scarred by people bearing the name Christian.

Hipster writer Donald Miller and his friends had a similar experience in their college years as the few Christ followers on Reed College's campus years ago. He recounts a story in *Blue Like Jazz* of his friends apologising to the masses of adamantly non-Christian peers for atrocities committed in the name of Christ. It was a hugely healing experience for both sides according to his telling.

I haven't done the same exact thing, but I've adjusted course in my life to make sure my actions are actually representative of a follower of Jesus. Sadly, I've seen several of my peers from high school who responded by tossing off all the trappings of Christianity including the Christ who was referenced but not represented in many of their experiences. The other extreme, those who dug into the trenches of legalism and nominal representation of Christianity, are also present among my generation, none of which I want to be like.

I want people to see me as a follower of Jesus, and I try to make decisions that demonstrate that obviously to those around me. I've also carefully chosen role models who are dedicated Jesus followers who encourage me in how to adjust my own life to grow as a Jesus follower like my professor Dr. Pothen.

Most university professors develop a following of devotees, and Dr. Pothen considered herself different. "Other professors have disciples," she told a group of students one day, "but I don't. I have dissenters." She thought this was funny because she was teaching students to think critically and not to regurgitate what she said. Just a couple years later, I'm told she described me as "the quintessential Pothen child," which I consider quite a high compliment.

I've always preferred the following role over the leading one, but part of leading is being a good follower. My friend Beckie explained that to me one day when she had come over for tea and brought me a little toy sheep that lived on my windowsill the next several years.

When Beckie pulled it out of her bag, she explained to me that it had a double meaning.

"You are a sheep of the Good Shepherd, and he will always care for you, but you are also a shepherd of other little sheep who are the students in your care."

She encouraged me to keep the sheep as a reminder that I was always cared for as a follower of Jesus but that I also had the sacred responsibility to care for those who follow me.

I love my students; I call them my children because they mean so much to me. I also am nervous by the idea that they are following me. I love the image of me being a follower of Jesus, but sometimes I want to shoo away the people who follow after me. I'm going to fail them all someday, and that's a lot of pressure. I actually emphasise that to students a lot — and I use Scripture and Demon Hunter songs to back me up. During a chapel talk at BFA, I quoted 2 Timothy 2:13 (if we are faithless, he remains faithful) and the chorus of the Demon Hunter song "I Will Fail You." I think you get the connection: there is a better person to put your faith in than me, but if you look at my example, I will do my best to point you to Jesus despite my failures.

I was hearkening back to Dr. Pothen's desire to have dissenters over disciples. I did realise though that there was a benefit to followers if I used my leadership to point them to Jesus and make sure they knew I was a thoroughly flawed individual.

After several years of teaching, I'm dissenting from Dr. Pothen's choice of word and prefer to say that I create disruptors. The students who congregated around my doorway to eat their lunch one year referred to themselves as "The Hewettian Order," but they were completely self-organised and continued eating there and joking about that association with me during the year I was away for my visa totalisation. They disrupted the flow of foot traffic through the hallway during lunch (which generally only stopped me from getting into my classroom the year they formed when I was there). They also made small but intentional disruptions to the status quo in life and faith and lots of other things.

Significantly, they don't do all the same things that I would do. They would leave my class energised to find new ways of understanding how loving Jesus and loving others transforms their daily lives. One of them told me that her desire to love God and love others that was kindled in my class led her to want to set up additional ways to allow high school students to engage and encourage middle school students in our school. This obviously is not something I would do because I avoid nearly every need to engage with middle school students.

Another, Maggie, earned the association as my "mini me" due to her round face, square glasses, and affinity for nerd culture. However, quality disruptor that she is, Maggie eagerly jumped into opportunities to educate people on the conflict in Palestine. This is a personal passion since she spent several formative years living in that country, but the zeal to convince others to change their minds on this nuanced geo-political conflict is far beyond any interest I have in politics.

Maggie is generally more interested in politics than I am (I strangely seem to attract the politically zealous students to conversations in my classroom despite my consistent vocal complaints about my distaste for politics), and she's also considerably more keen on the discipline of science. I've had conversations with her about what she might do with her life, and among the many options, a consistent potential in her high school years was to become a coroner. This would have been an opportunity for her to love Jesus and integrate her faith into a unique career. While my own high school Bible teacher was also our school science teacher and my supervisor is a science teacher turned Bible teacher, my preference for the field of literature is clear to all students. Maggie is a strong disruptor of my patterns — finding ways to see how science lights up her understanding of faith while I'm always defaulting to literary examples. She's clearly following Jesus over me despite the fact she ended up a writer. I would be devastated if anyone called her a "Ms. Hewett follower" rather than a Jesus follower.

She would always readily engage in opportunities to have tea at my house or tacos with me at the Bryans' house. My last week in Germany before moving to New Zealand at the start of Maggie's senior year, she and her former roommate Leah joined me at the Bryans' during my last Taco Tuesday for a while. As usual for a Taco Tuesday, there was lots of laughter, hot sauce, and Narnia involved, but the ride home quickly became somber.

It was my goodbye to Maggie and Leah as I'd be flying to New Zealand the next day, and I couldn't ignore that. Maggie's family had recently moved to Kandern, and I expected to see her in a little over a year, but it was still hard to know I'd miss out on baking cookies with her through her last year as a BFA student. Once we pulled up to her house, Maggie reluctantly got out of the car and I opened the front door to give her a last hug.

"Ms. Hewett," Maggie asked me very seriously, "What does a mini-me do when the mega-me moves to New Zealand?"

"She thrives," I responded with no hesitation.

12

On Stories

I'm not sure what first intrigued me about the writing of Elie Wiesel, but there was something insatiable about my curiosity by the time I had to select my undergraduate thesis topic. I wanted to understand the thread that ran through all of his collected writings, so I chose to look at the first three and last three novels published at the time of my studies. I wrote about how the only way to avoid madness from suffering was through storytelling. I suppose it was inevitable I'd write the story of my suffering before going mad (or perhaps going mad through it depending on who you ask).

I read through a lot of Wiesel in university which led to the retelling of humans needing connection after trauma and sharing their lives through hurt becoming an important truth for me to inhabit as I found myself stuck in a hospital bed less than two years after turning in my thesis. In so many ways, my reading and research on suffering and storytelling emotionally prepared me for that experience as I deeply understood how I would need to share what I was experiencing in order to heal from it. I had a blog for updating North American friends about my European adventures, but I quickly shifted platforms and perspective as I wrote about my immediate physical recovery from my hospital bed.

Soon after I left the hospital, a friend recommended that I write a memoir sooner rather than later because it would become a different story the longer I waited. She was right, and this book has certainly shifted over the years since I started drafting it. I've learned a lot about storytelling and sharing stories. For example, I've learned that rather than pontificating on cultural values surrounding storytelling, readers would be more interested to know about how my childhood best friend Kara and I used to hide in corners of the playground and pull out notebooks to write fantasy stories because we loved reading about Narnia and Middle Earth and wanted to invent different lands with interesting characters who we could share with each other.

Unfortunately, neither of us was particularly creative in our world building, nor did we have much insight in how to craft a compelling plot. Kara went on to become a faculty physician in Duke's Special Infant Care Clinic because she's a boss like that, and I stopped posting short stories on Elfwood. Praise the Lord that website mysteriously disappeared from the internet with all of my angsty poetry and terrible fantasy fiction. While Kara shifted her attention to life saving skills through firefighter and paramedic training, I dug deeper into the written worlds of Elie Wiesel, Chaim Potok, Virginia Woolf, and Ursula LeGuin among others. I also got a bachelors and master's degree, a teacher's license, and moved internationally to teach Bible and English to high school missionary kids. I also read a lot of John Green and some Rick Riordan.

Backing up a bit, my affection for stories started when my parents taught me to read. By the time I was learning to read chapter books, my dad let me read *The Chronicles of Narnia* with him as my bed time stories. He'd tried with my sister a couple of years before, but the talking animals freaked her out, so she found different books to read. I was enthralled, and I loved following along with the text as my dad read the bite sized chapters and tucked me into bed. I'd stare at the illustrations on each page as they came up, and sometimes he'd let me read a few pages to him. My favourite days were when I managed to sneak an extra chapter in by tipping the page away from my dad as I read. I'd wrap up the scene and start the next paragraph in the same breath, careful that adult eyes couldn't see the clear page break as I started the next chapter and extended both my bedtime and the adventure in Narnia. Those evening story times were formative experiences for me as I learned about other worlds and how humans were made to interact with each other. I learned empathy and the power of allusions through the craft of C. S. Lewis.

Years later when I was in grad school, I discovered two of the kids I babysat had never read the series. I begged their parents to let me read Narnia aloud to their kids. I'd reread them when taking an undergraduate class on Lewis and fell in love on a deeper level. I wanted to be part of sharing them with these kids I cared about. We worked out a weekly system where I read to the two boys in a back office while their parents attended the sermon at church. While the younger one struggled to focus for that time, the middle school boy was so enthralled with the storytelling, he asked me to read him *The Lord of the Rings* aloud once we finished *The Chronicles of Narnia*. I happily obliged, but we quickly realised one series was written to be read aloud to children while the other had some serious drag in the forest descriptions. It was a formative experience of a different kind as I shared that reading journey with the kid who would become one of the first people to join my support team when I became a missionary. His parents made it very clear that the kid was the one who chose to give of his allowance because he saw such value in how I lived out Jesus' values through my work and life and reading habits.

Five years into my teaching, I found another young person who hadn't read through Narnia. She was a voracious reader, and I again found myself begging someone to let me read the books aloud. We only made it through two, but it was while she was sitting on my couch with a mug of tea as I was reflecting about my first experience reading Narnia that it occurred to me that my dad knew I'd read past the chapter end.

"I learned to read with this series. My dad would read them aloud as bedtime stories," I told her excitedly, "And I was such a clever kid — I used to sneak extra chapters in by turning the book away from him until I turned the page. It was especially difficult for me because I usually loved to spend time staring at the details of the illustrations, and I had to try to multitask in my six-year-old brain as I took in the words and image somewhat simultaneously." Suddenly I paused, realising there was no way that my six-year-old brain actually had the capacity to do that with any measure of subtly.

What a jaw dropping moment to discover in my late twenties that I wasn't as clever as I thought as a six-year-old sneaking an extra chapter before bed. Of course he knew, and of course he loved watching me sound out words and point out allusions between Aslan and Jesus. He loved it as much as I loved listening to the young people I read to talk about how they saw faith puzzles worked out between the text and their own lives.

A year before I left Germany, I had one more opportunity with a student to read Narnia aloud. This student was a TA for another teacher during one of my prep periods and would often have mindless office tasks like hole punching, stapling, or filing on Wednesdays. We coordinated that once a week I'd make sure to be in the office and read to her while she did her tasks. Introducing her to Narnia was such a joy, and it brought a little bit of life to the empty staff room while she made her way through the day's duties. Within a few months of moving to New Zealand, I found a friend who hadn't heard of Narnia, and the pattern remains the same as I await the opportunity to read the series together.

Narnia is compelling for a lot of reasons, but it's something I've loved sharing with others. The same student who got Ray Lubeck's quote tattooed on her arm started a podcast where she talks with friends about the valuable life lessons for adults embedded in children's literature. She started with episodes for each book in the Narnia series. She also shared life with me and invited me as a guest on a couple podcast episodes. We share life stories with each other as we talk about scenes in Narnia, and our conversations are deep and enriching. There's a reference in the next chapter from the climax of *The Silver Chair* which most people consider their least favourite book of the series. If you listen to the podcast episode, you'll hear my passionate defence of the text in response to her insistence the whole book is a fever dream that makes no sense.

By the time Lissy was recording those podcasts, she knew a lot of my life as related through analogies of Narnian characters. I knew elements of her story through the same way; our conversation about the points of tension we each have with our "perfect" older sisters is greatly enhanced by our discussion of Lucy's temptation at the wizard's spell book. We also have portions of each others' lives that we've related through biblical narratives. She's a Timothy to my Paul, and Elisha to my Elijah, and a whole bunch of other individuals we each relate to. Two thirds of the Bible is stories, and that's because humans relate through story. Narratives are more compelling than lists. When I have questions in life, I ponder the lives of biblical and literary heroes and look for principles through the lives recorded and shared with me. Sometimes I look at the stories of people around me for the same reason.

Sometimes people look to me for encouragement from my story. While I was on sabbatical, a former student reached out to me out of the blue to talk to me about her story, my story, understanding story in general, and how faith weaves into that. And disability. That was involved in the conversation too. What an encouragement that conversation was to me.

Sarah has a totally different disability than I do, but we both have physical limitations. We had a lovely chat, and while we didn't solve ableism in the world, we had some good laughs and both found some important confidence in our understanding of ourselves as humans made in the image of God. What actually is most beautiful about the way that Sarah and I shared stories with each other is that we don't live our lives focused on our disability. She's got this passion and training for theatre production, and I love watching her bounce around the US reflecting on the ideas of home, place, and identity. Every few weeks or months, Sarah will post a link on her Facebook to a new blog post she's written reflecting on being a TCK who grew up across six countries, living in transition, or what it's like to create a sense of home.

A handful of the students in Sarah's graduating class were passionate about reading, writing, and for some reason conversations with me. I've stayed quite close with a few of them, and I love watching the way they use their stories to process the struggles and celebrations in their lives. The blog posts aren't frequent, but they are certainly deep. For someone who writes a weekly update about my own life, I'm actually quite reticent to read other regular bloggers, but when Sarah or Phoebe post an update, I will drop whatever I'm doing to read it. I think what compels me most about their sharing is the way they write about the moment and don't brag about their flash upbringing in the Middle East or how wild their life adventures are. You know Sarah is extra special for this relatability and humility because her precious brother is the exact opposite. He is one of those stereotypical TCKs who accidentally comes off as aloof and pretentious for starting sentences mid-conversation with things like, "During my high school class trip to Rome..." Grounded and humble, Sarah writes with the longing to connect places and remember old homes.

Her stories are of commuting between the theatre and her apartment, noticing how the same sun sets in different places and casts light into the corners of her soul across continents. She writes beautiful sentences that are prime for connecting anyone to her thought process by sharing the surface stories of her life as the entry into her heart. I'm intensely conscious of the fact that I asked for her permission to share my overlap with her story, and she generously agreed without hesitation. As I meander through writing my own memoir, I wonder why my story is any more compelling than Sarah's. The truth is, it's not. We both have a rich and beautiful life experience, and people have plenty to gain by engaging with each of us as storytellers who will intentionally write as accessibly as possible.

When I set out to compile the important stories of my life, I wanted to encourage as many people as possible. Years ago, I joked with a friend that I really only had like six good teacher stories and that four of them were about the same student. The reality is, I have a story for every circumstance; I've selected an intentional few to put into print here. Each student I named in the text gave their consent for me to share their story as it overlapped with mine, and it led to several conversations about my perspective in our connections. It also forced me to remember carefully as I wanted to honestly and thoughtfully represent others. Each young person had the opportunity to give feedback, and they generously shared helpful critique or encouragements. I was also intentional in choosing student stories that reflected on a purposeful theme or topic. When I set out to write a whole book about myself, I really resisted the idea of a chronological narrative of my accident and recovery. I wanted this telling of my life story to represent a fuller picture.

In the original draft of this memoir, I also determined to have equal stories related to my life before my disability as those after. I wanted to demonstrate clearly how interesting and valuable and worth celebrating my life was before disability; I wanted to prove to myself that my story was worth reading if it wasn't centred around this accident. Now I can release the word counts and attempts to balance what was before or after

January 18, 2014. This collection of stories you're reading now is my attempt to reflect on how I've seen God show up in my life.

I stepped away from that previous structure to use a lot more fluidity as I write stream of consciousness sections and attempt to show more of myself in each story.

One more throwback story for you here begins with a character introduced into my life when I was in the third grade. My sister's best friend's dad married this woman from New Jersey who is a gifted writer. There are a lot of ways to describe her role and relationship in my life, but I usually just call her my friend Shirley. Shirley described me as "ten going on forty" when she first met me. Now as I am less than ten years from turning forty, I act a lot closer to ten than to forty. In my early teenage years, Shirley found out that I wanted to be a writer. I'm not sure how, but she somehow got my parents to agree to let her take me to a regional writers gathering one day.

We had a good distance to drive and talk together on the way out, and I remember being full of anticipation of meeting more real writers and learning all kinds of information about the craft. At the time, Shirley was writing a crime novel, and while she let me pick a lot of the workshops, we also went to some key ones relevant to her genre. In particular, she was interested in learning some details from the former police officer who was offering insights in how to write accurate descriptions of police stations and arrest processes and the ins and outs of the legal system.

"When you get arrested, you're going to have the police speak to you this way — this lady knows what I'm talking about," the presenter cut himself off as he pointed to Shirley who was nodding along knowingly to his descriptions. To be honest, I can't remember the exact detail he was sharing about the process; I just remember this was suddenly the moment I learned that Shirley had been arrested. This woman is full of great stories, and I got to hear extras in the car ride home after some of the things brought up at the writing workshop. To this day, we laugh about how my parents put me in her charge for the day.

What stands out to me most about that whole experience with Shirley is not actually learning about her past (though she has a fascinating life story). What stands out to me is that she shared her life and passion with me and encouraged my development as a storyteller. Shirley is one of the people who has been my biggest advocates through life to hone my craft. Her pithy repeated "academic Laura" comment written through the first draft of this book show how much she cares about me presenting the most honest and intentional version of myself through my writing.

The shortcoming of writing is that you can revise indefinitely, so the final version of this text will still have weaknesses. However, I do know that the stories included will have their value shine a little bit brighter through the revision process as I add layers to my narratives.

On Prayer

According to my Goodreads shelf, I read seventy books related to prayer in the span of four years. I'm not saying that to sound cool or like some kind of expert. I'm saying that for some context to this story. Prayer has become a significant part of my life through a pretty embarrassing and vulnerable catalyst. Those books represent a lot of painful growth in my spiritual life. I read them in order to learn how to pray well enough to stop praying for the coworker who I had asked to pray for me once he told me that God was punishing me with a disability. That's a convoluted sentence, so let's back up a bit and start this story in the fall of 2016.

My student Nick was absolutely delightful to have in class. He was full of life and distractions and energy and passion for learning about the Gospel and theology. A sharp young man who grew up in the Holy Land, Nick was the only student who caught what it meant when I dropped a Greek word in class, explained the reference to the Septuagint, and explained the Hebrew connection. We went off and soared across the theological implications of the incarnation leaving most of his peers behind (except the one other kid who spoke some Hebrew).

He also really loved harmless pranks that would make everyone laugh. After a presentation in my class, he left the USB connecting his remote to my computer plugged in, and it took me ages to figure out why my slides were possessed and advancing on their own. When he heard about a peer in another class jokingly referring to me as "Mother" because I built my classroom rapport by referring to my class as my children, Nick made it his life goal to get as many students as possible to call me "Mother." I was mildly annoyed at the start, but nearly eight years later there are still a handful of twenty-somethings around the world who refer to me as "Mother Hewett," and I can't help but have a special spot for them in my heart.

Nick and his roommate were two of the first kids to take me up on the after school snacks offer, and soon that became regular dinner nights mixed into the after school cookie making at my house though his junior and senior year. I don't know how many kilos of *pico de gallo* were consumed in my house through that period, but I promise you it was a lot. Nick is a lovable kid, and he bonded with a lot of the staff members at BFA, but I was probably among his top four favourite staff members.

At the very least, I was one of the four staff members who were still at BFA years later when Nick was getting married who live streamed his wedding together. Because Nick got married on a lovely Saturday afternoon in Wyoming, we stayed up until 1am on a Sunday morning in Germany to stream the service with terrible internet connection. There was a massive thunderstorm in Kandern that night, and my porch had incredible views. Since Lauren and Emily lived next door where we were watching the wedding later that night, we gathered outside with Robbie, who was visiting from England, and the other staff member who knew Nick to sit and watch nature's show as we kept ourselves awake. I parked myself in front of the mailbox, and, for some reason, Emily stopped after bringing out just one chair and stood in the door with Lauren and Robbie while this other person sat next to me.

What a show. I love thunderstorms. I *love* thunderstorms. Anytime the sky gets dark with rain laden clouds, I get excited anticipating the smells and sounds and sights about to come. The staccato smacks of heavy raindrops hitting the ground in quick succession, the unpredictable flashes lighting up the sky, counting the miles by seconds until the thunder confirms with loud echoes for my ears what my eyes saw for a moment. This was one of the greatest thunderstorms, and my heart ached to get up and dance in the rain. My legs were stuck in my wheelchair. My body suddenly felt uncomfortable.

Ask them to pray for you to dance in the rain.

What a weird thought. *No, that's a silly thing to do,* I told myself and carried on the following internal monologue to convince myself why that was a bad idea: I've had conversations with Lauren and Emily and Robbie about walking again, but this dude sitting next to me is kinda a jerk. He once told one of my students that she wasn't a real Christian because he disagreed with a statement she made on a secondary theological issue; he also hangs out with a family that once tried to get me fired.

I had plenty of reasons loaded why I didn't feel safe asking him to pray for me. I convinced myself I could ask my friends to pray for me later — after he left, maybe I'd have a moment that felt like a natural opening to ask for prayer.

At that point in my life, I'd been in a wheelchair for six and a half year, so asking people to pray for me every single ordinary day felt weird. Sometimes you just gotta be content with what God's given you and wait for the right moments. I shouldn't hijack all the moments for attention on my miraculous physical healing. That was kinda the rundown of the thought and the logical justification to ignore that Holy Spirit nudge to ask for prayer right then.

Then something weird happened.

Okay, **Naaman.**

My body resonated with the sassy reprimand. There is no other way to describe the sensation — trust me; I've tried. This is the single weirdest God/Holy Spirit/Supernatural experience I've ever had. Somehow in that holy moment as the rain poured down, the instant I determined not to ask this guy sitting next to me to pray for my miraculous healing allowing me to dance in the rain, my body *resonated* with holy sass from above as God dumped the story of Naaman the Syrian on me simultaneous with the parallels of that moment all dripping with divine sarcasm.

For those unfamiliar, there's a story in the Old Testament in 2 Kings 5 about this Syrian general who has a skin disease. He's got an Israeli slave girl working in his home, and she pipes up, "Oh, we've got a guy in Israel who can heal you; his name is Elisha." Powerful general that he is, his king sends Namaan into enemy territory to get healed, and the Israelite king freaks out thinking it's a provocation for war. Elisha gets word and is like, "I got this, bro." When Naaman turns up at his house, Elisha calmly says, "Go wash in the Jordan River, and you'll be healed."

"Gross," Naaman replies, "Don't I have better rivers at home in Syria? That one is nasty."

Elisha can shrug his shoulders and walk away. Naaman's servant eventually convinces him that since he's come all this way, he might as well try to dip in the Israelites' dirty river before returning home. Naaman does it, and he's instantly healed. It's a wild time, and there are some other details about Elisha's servant and false pretences of payment, but the gist God impressed on my heart in that moment on August 1, 2020 was that I was Naaman, this dude sitting next to me was the Jordan River, and my friends standing by the door were my Syrian rivers. I wanted the people I liked to be the ones to pray for me, to be involved in any miraculous healing. Actually, more honestly, I wasn't going to be embarrassed to ask them to pray knowing that other people had been praying with no major miracle in the past six and a half years. I believe those prayers mattered, but I had tempered expectations over that long span of time.

I was a mess for days after that refusal and spiritual rebuttal. When we watched Nick's wedding ceremony later that night, I was seated on a couch next to this guy, and my leg was spasming uncontrollably as if to shout to the room that I had disobeyed the Lord and was supposed to have asked for healing.

The next afternoon, Lauren found me alone at the picnic table outside our house and asked me if I was doing okay. I admitted that I was supposed to ask the group to pray for a miracle that night and hadn't done it. "Ah, yeah, it seemed like something was off with you last night," she nodded. Then, she put her hand on me and asked the Lord for a full and miraculous, instantaneous miracle. I thanked her and then sheepishly added that I'd actually felt unnaturally convicted that I was supposed to ask that other guy to pray for me. She nodded again and said something like, "That makes sense." Lauren was by my side for a lot of weirdness starting that moment and carrying through the next year. She gave me the grace to never question my sanity even though I regularly did.

Later that day, I shared the weird events with Maggie who promptly insisted that I text him to ask him to pray for me. I squirmed with discomfort as I pulled out my phone to send a message along the lines of, "You know that guy Naaman in the Bible? Well, I was supposed to ask you to pray for me to dance in the rain, and I didn't. So, I am now." Then, because I'd been a jerk to him at a party a couple weeks before when he tried to include me in a conversation by asking my middle name but I didn't want to engage with the arrogant jerk and told him that was personal information and left the party — *that was happening outside my kitchen window* — I added to the text, "My middle name is Diane." I meant it as a peace offering, but I also didn't give him any context, and I have no idea if any of that message made sense in his head when he read it.

There were a lot of connected events in my mind that really would have read like a jumbled mess to most people, so to this day, I don't know if my poor initial communication on that day had any impact on what played out over the next few months and years.

He responded almost immediately with his middle name and an assent to pray, but when no further details came, I clarified that I needed him to show up at my house and tell me to my face to stand up and walk in the name of Jesus.

This is crazy person talk.

Legit, who does this? Crazy people. I am crazy people.

But the guy agreed.

We arranged a time, or so I thought, and he didn't show. I followed up with increasing anxiety over the oddity of the situation, and when he said he'd come sometime on the following day, I asked Maggie if she was free. I honestly didn't feel safe having this intense encounter alone. I'd already felt weird enough asking him to pray, and I kinda knew part of me would back down if it was an interaction with him alone. Maggie was my accountability to follow through on this Holy Spirit nudge to ask homeboy to pray for me. To pray that I would miraculously walk again. To ask me to stand up and walk in the name of Jesus.

When he texted me that he was on his way, I made sure to tell Maggie so she had enough time to get to my house. We were sitting at my picnic table when he pulled his van into the dirt parking in front of my house. The air was thick. Or as Maggie and I would later come to describe it, thiccc — with three c's for the presence of the Trinity. The whole town was blanketed in that holy feeling you sometimes get when walking into ancient temples or powerful worship gatherings. The table was positioned under the shade of the tree on the hot, summer day, and I was sitting with my back to the driveway at the end of the table. Maggie sat near me on the side closest to the tree; homeboy came over and stood between us.

After some awkward greetings, he put his hand on my shoulder and prayed, "God, if it's your will, please let Laura walk someday."

My heart sank.

I knew I had to clarify the request.

"Um, thanks, thank you. I know this is really weird, but could you pray without any caveats for God?"

"What do you mean? I didn't give any caveats," his semi-southern accent feigned innocence.

Okay, hold up, that's me reading into his motives, and that's not fair. This story is about to get weird. Buckle up for the wild parts, and I will do my best to describe the facts, but I've got to give this warning that my experiences are always going to have a subjective slant. My perceptions of this event impacted my emotions and subsequent responses. Maggie and I went through every detail of this interaction afterwards, many times, and we were completely in sync with our perceptions, but I will still do my best to differentiate between fact and interpretations in order to give you a glimpse into my raw emotions as I lived through these events.

"What do you mean? I didn't give any caveats," he shifted his weight, and I swallowed trying to think about how to best explain myself.

There's a theological camp that says you shouldn't demand things from God so all our requests should be submitted under God's will. There is an equally passionate group on the other side of the issue that says we claim healing in the name of Jesus. I fall into neither. I absolutely want my prayers to be in line with God's will, and I absolutely believe there is healing power in the name of Jesus, and I have no idea why I had this burning in my gut that told me this guy was adding that line at the end of his prayer not to be theologically honouring to God but as an act of disbelief in the healing power of the name of Jesus. So with that understanding in my mind — whether right or wrong — I responded, "You added 'if it's your will,' to give God an out. Can you pray again but just ask that I stand up and walk in the name of Jesus?"

To his credit, he did.

Nothing happened, but somehow, in that moment, all three of us now knew there was something bigger at play, and we weren't done.

Homeboy walked behind me and sat down at the picnic table opposite to Maggie. We had a light theological conversation. No, that's not true. We had a heavy theological conversation with tentative sentences as we each tested out how the other would respond to what we were presenting about the power of healing, the Lord's timing, the voice of the Holy Spirit, and why I was so convinced that it was important this guy pray for me with the conviction that God could instantly heal me whether or not the healing happened. When I looked in his eyes, all I could see was fear. My interpretation — and I know this isn't fact, it's just an interpretation, but it exerted massive influence on my reactions — was that he had heard the Holy Spirit speak clearly to him that he was supposed to be a part of my miraculous healing story, and it freaked him out more than anything in his entire life. At one point in the conversation, responding to a comment from Maggie, homeboy said the words, "I don't know what Laura has to learn about suffering and lamentation before God will heal her."

I fact checked that line with Maggie multiple times because that sentence was a turning point in my life and will come up again later. I shut down emotionally in that moment. I felt that man wasn't interested in being invited into my healing story, and he had just implied that God wasn't going to heal me until I'd learned my lesson about suffering. Years later, I can view each person in that conversation with a great deal more compassion, but in the moment, my vision was myopic and locked on my own hurt from that statement. Our conversation carried on, remaining intense, until we actually tried to have me stand and take a few steps holding his hands.

I've done this before with other people — walking with someone holding my hands is not particularly impressive. Also worth noting, my left leg was spasming pretty violently beyond normal conditions throughout this entire encounter. Also, *also* worth noting, because we weren't friends, these conditions were not known to this individual. He didn't know I could take any steps at all because he'd never seen me out of my wheelchair.

I turned my chair around to angle towards him and the driveway before I put my hands on his forearms to stand. I managed to pull myself upright and get my heels on the ground; I wasn't wearing my braces. The left leg settled enough, but I had him on my right for the extra support. Maggie walked a step behind, lagging on my left. We walked to the edge of the property, crossed the street, and carried on around the corner to the entrance of the supermarket a contextually impressive fifty metres away. There were a couple of options at this point, and I was pretty fed up with this individual. By then, we'd talked in circles for probably an hour before this attempt at some physical prompting of a miracle, and I couldn't shake the sense that this guy was holding back something — his belief was my best guess. Again, that was my interpretation which heavily coloured my emotional response in the moment. I also knew that for those few steps we'd taken, I'd been completely supported by him, and I was ready to give up on this guy who I had already so harshly condemned in my heart. I didn't like feeling so vulnerable and dependent on him physically.

"Where do we go?" I asked Maggie, knowing she was in sync with the Holy Spirit in this moment, and my energy was flagging due to my irritation with this guy.

"We can turn around and go back."

As I turned, I kept homeboy to the roadside and shifted my support to have him holding onto my left arm. This meant Maggie was a step ahead on my right — where I needed the support because of my spasming left leg. Maggie clocked the whole thing; Maggie took a step back.

"You need to trust him," she told me.

I swore loudly.

I took a step forward without any support on my right, and I stumbled. Homeboy managed to catch my right arm and stood facing me before laughing, "Now we're going to tango."

I was beyond annoyed at this point, and I kept my words even and terse as I told the man, "You have to lead me."

He had no clue what he was doing, but he took short steps backwards and my feet followed his from the firehouse across the street back to my picnic table where I sat myself in the wheelchair in exhaustion and frustration.

"Well, I have raw chicken in my front seat that I should get home," he told Maggie and I after our long, hot summer afternoon of awkward.

As he drove away, Maggie and I reflected on the whole conversation. I mentioned the terror in his eyes, and she agreed she'd seen it as well and interpreted it exactly the same way. From our perspective, as we shared our sensations and promptings and interpretations, Maggie and I had felt the identical thing independently. Our guess was that homeboy felt it too, but he wasn't interested in participating in the miraculous work of God that day.

I know what Maggie thought because she shared it with me in that moment. Homeboy never gave me that courtesy when I asked for clarification.

The night of that fateful interaction, I went to sleep pretty upset. I woke up at 3:30am with a burning conviction to pray for this guy. *"I'm about to wrestle with him,"* I felt like God was telling me. I want to be super cautious in this phrasing because while I felt like I knew that or heard that from God, it wasn't an audible voice; it was a reason to be startled awake in the middle of the night, so I spent the next six hours praying intensely for this guy I barely knew. Then I wrote the poem "Bless Me" which I later shared on my blog and was a catalyst for the publication of my first collection of poems. That morning when I wrote it, though, I got out of bed with this strange conviction that God wanted to give me good things, that he wanted to heal me fully and miraculously in a way that only he could get the credit for. At that moment in my mind, homeboy was an inconvenient means to an end. The end was me glorifying God and dancing in the rain.

The next night, I woke up at 3:30am again, prompted to pray. I barely slept more than three hours that night.

This would continue through the next six months until I started setting a timer to pray for him for a full hour each night before I went to bed each night to help me to sleep through the night better.

Just a couple of days after this inciting picnic table incident, at Maggie's insistence, I messaged this guy and told him some of his words were hurtful and that I'd like to give him a chance to clear things up. He never replied. I tried again a few days later with the same silence in response.

This made me understandably annoyed. I was angry. I was mad, and out of my hurt and irritability, I unfortunately was quick to bash this guy when he came up in conversation. One disappointing example was in a sort of discipleship group I was leading with four other young staff members. I let off a string of insults and swear words that makes me blush to think about. I actually had to text an apology to our group chat the next day. Shortly after that, I was talking to my friend Chris about my irritation with this overall situation, and one of the young staff from the discipleship group who was present at my tirade was in the room with Chris and I that day. She and I had really only just started getting to know each other, but she interjected that based on the facts she knew, my emotions and words seemed reasonable.

"Maybe, but that's not the kind of person who I want to be," I responded. "I *am* mad at him, and I *am* hurt by the situation, but that doesn't give me license to insult him to a roomful of people behind his back."

Chris thought I was overreacting about the whole situation. Chris is a really good friend who had a fancy espresso machine in his classroom, so naturally, I spent a lot of time there with a coffee in hand during our common prep period. He is also a really smart dude, so every time I would rant about something related to this situation, he could tell I was holding back certain information. He'd offer the best advice he could, but it usually wasn't that helpful because I'd only ranted about one sliver of the problem and left out a whole lot of detail and context in my blind rage. From inside my body, I felt like I was growing increasingly unhinged as I couldn't shake the prompting to pray for this guy who had barely registered on my radar of existence for the previous few years he'd been on staff at our school. For someone who I rarely interacted with, I was so frustrated that people kept bringing him up to me *all the time*. Or at least it felt like it in the moment.

I remember having dinner with some good friends one week when something with this guy had come up again. "He seems to come up a lot lately," my friend mentioned casually.

"I know. It's *disturbing*, isn't it?"

"No," he chuckled, "It's just interesting. I don't know that it means anything."

Truth be told, I would have loved the easy answer of someone interpreting this whole ordeal as a disturbing mess. It would have been easier to shut it down. But all my friends kept telling me I should keep praying for this guy who was so obviously a wounded person. Two empaths I taught described his physical presence when he entered a room as like being "shot in the gut" or "stabbed in the chest." Homeboy *radiated* hurt everywhere he went. Due to my lack of sleep and frustration with the unshakeable conviction to spend hours in prayer for this guy, I started buying up books on spiritual warfare and prayer to hurry this ordeal to an end. I figured if I learned how to pray better, God would end the conviction. Lest anyone miss the glaring irony: I thought this inconvenience in my life would end if I learned the lesson God was trying to teach me about prayer.

By complete random happenstance, homeboy found a book I had purchased on spiritual warfare prayer which I had left on my picnic table while I was away for a few minutes. By even wilder happenstance, he later encountered me alone at the table reading it.

"I noticed that book earlier," he'd been flipping through it and would have found it impossible to ignore my green pen underlining, annotations, and stars in the margin. "Is it any good?"

"Yeah, it is," I replied hesitantly. I was intensely uncomfortable at the notion of him reading my notes in the margin — some of which related to him, others which were just personal and private.

"What's something good from it? Read me a bit."

I flipped to the double starred passage I'd read earlier that related a story almost identical to the theological untruth he'd said to me six weeks before. I read out how the author shared a young friend's misled conviction that the bad in his life was a punishment from God, and the author's response that God does not inflict suffering on us in his anger and that Jesus has taken the punishment for our sins so that we don't have to.

Homeboy nodded along, "Yeah, that's true; that's good stuff."

My jaw dropped.

"Uh, but that's exactly what you told me at the beginning of August. You implied God wasn't going to heal me until I learned my lesson about suffering."

"What? I'd never say that. I don't believe that."

His facial expression was something resembling incredulous; my interpretation was that he was faking it. My facial expression matched; I was most certainly not faking it.

"Why didn't you say something if that's what you thought I was implying?" He asked me.

"I texted you to ask for clarification. *Twice.*" My voice was tense, and my pulse was elevated.

"Oh, I didn't think those messages required a response."

My breathing was shallow, and my brain got foggy here. My body attempted to regulate the physiological responses as I sorted through questions like, *Were my messages unclear? Wait, did he really not say that in our conversation before? Have I misread this situation entirely? Am I a different kind of crazy than I expected? Should I apologise to Chris for all those times I snapped at him over not taking my frustrations seriously? Have I blown this out of proportion? Why can't I sleep then?*

We actually carried on an increasingly uncomfortable conversation out loud as I told him I'd bought this book because I hadn't slept for the past six weeks as the Lord kept prompting me to pray for him. He said some rude and cagey things, and I was still reeling about the possibility that I drastically misunderstood our last interaction while increasingly disliking him in this interaction. I called Maggie up as soon as possible after that and asked her what she remembered of our August conversation with him.

"Oh, he definitely said, and I quote, 'I don't know what Laura has to learn about suffering and lamentation before God will heal her,' and it was for sure implying that your lack of healing was your fault and wouldn't happen until you'd learned your lesson." She also had a few more direct quotes in her memory that were pretty offensively ableist and theologically problematic.

My anger was amplified after this, and I probably needed a good cool off period without engaging in any ministry, but that just wasn't the life I was living. My irritability leaked over into a discipleship group call with a handful of alumni, three of whom had had this guy as an RA at some point during their years in the dorm. One of them was Nick. Nick whose wedding I watched sitting next to this guy the night my world turned upside down. Nick married this lovely girl Isabel that fateful day, and while I have not yet met Isabel in person, but she is on my list of absolute favourite humans on the planet. I have so many good things to say about Isabel, and they all start with this first interaction that demonstrated incredible bravery, humility, Christ-like character, and discernment. Only having heard from Nick about me, Isabel was given the impression that my character was one of great wisdom and maturity. Nick may be one to exaggerate, but he also respects me a lot and had communicated to his new wife that I was deserving of such respect. She sat in the background of our group call, engaged in something else but listening as I "led" a discipleship call where I derailed a conversation with yet another tirade about this jerk face who'd insulted me and how I was now burdened to pray for him constantly and was losing significant hours of precious sleep. We eventually got back on track, maybe, and the call ended.

Nick messaged the next day and said he and Isabel had been talking and praying about the situation. She told him the verse ringing in her head during my tirade was 1 Corinthians 13:1-2, "If I speak in the tongues of men and of angels, but have not love, I am a noisy gong or a clanging cymbal. And if I have prophetic powers, and understand all mysteries and all knowledge, and if I have all faith, so as to remove mountains, but have not love, I am nothing." Nick went on to say that if I wasn't able to love this guy and ask him to heal me, "then the miracle, successful or unsuccessful, is meaningless." He then said if this guy was not able to love, same deal, the miraculous healing would be meaningless. Nick and Isabel were totally right.

This couple is fully invested in my healing story, and there are lots of jokes in our message history related to the oddity of this situation. There are also several profound spiritual insights like that 1 Corinthians one about how I was not just being childish and rude in my hurtful comments about this guy, but I was lacking love, a fruit of the spirit God calls me to have. Jesus straight up commands it of his followers in John 13 and says the world will recognise us as disciples by how we love one another.

My relationship with Isabel is tied up in this mess, and it jump started the depth of a lot of our spiritual conversations; it became a catalyst for Nick to seek the Scriptures deeply and listen to the Holy Spirit more closely. Hear me very carefully, God did not inflict this situation on me and Nick and Isabel for the purposes of our growth. The three of us were already on a trajectory towards closer relationship with Jesus, and this is just the life we happen to live. I've had several subsequent calls with Isabel where she's shared insight and excitement about how she's growing and what she's hearing in prayer. This story revolves around prayer, and I've recommended several books to her after reading them on this wild learning adventure I'm on.

The first sentence of this chapter noted that I've hit seventy books in my prayer reading journey. I started tracking them on a separate list on Goodreads when I realised God was teaching me something broader and bigger than I'd initially seen. I can laugh with you now about the idea that I would stop having to pray for homeboy once I learned my lesson just as I laugh with nearly everyone I know about his implication that I can't walk because I haven't learned my lesson about suffering and lamentation. The list is a handy reference if someone asks me for a recommendation on a book related to prayer and they have a couple parameters — a short book, one that has pre-written prayers in it, one that's easily readable, or a throwback to a different framework of prayer. I've got options for all the prayer books. My former student Julia once asked me to write her a book on prayer distilling all the best parts of the books I'd read since she'd never get around to reading that many. For her, I'd do that someday, but I'm not done reading the books just yet. Not because I think I'll get to stop praying for this guy, but because there is something beautiful and intimate about prayer that I'm just scratching the surface of seventy books in.

Each book is different as an author shares some principles or insights; prayer is a simple yet diverse thing. When I write my blog each week, I ask people to pray for my healing. When I write my reflections on my accident each year, I write five specific prayer requests for myself and my healing journey. I believe every prayer matters, but at the same time, I have no idea what those prayers have actually accomplished.

For over four years I prayed daily for this guy who hurt me — that he would open his eyes, step into the Chacos of peace, and obey the Holy Spirit. Every day. I prayed for him every single day. For four years. I saw absolutely no change in his life. Actually, I saw him inflict more hurt on others in the community which was a bit awkward. I can't say what difference my prayers have made in his life, but I know the difference they have made in mine. Because I was forced to pray for this guy, I started to humanise him instead of demonise him in conversations. I had this whole running analogy about how he was like Prince Rillian trapped inside the Black Knight in the children's classic *The Silver Chair*. My interactions with the jerk who behaved like a soulless robot were the Black Knight moments, but, if I looked closely, I might catch a glimpse of Prince Rillian begging to be set free from the Green Lady's evil enchantment. I also started to look for the humanity in other people who came across as jerks.

I became significantly less judgmental of others over the course of the last few years. I started to see others as broken people in need of kindness; I grew in compassion. I began intentionally offering affirmations to those around me to build people up rather than ignoring the hurts they might be hiding just under the surface.

There are plenty of blank spaces and question marks when it comes to things like why that guy, why that summer, why that phrase or insight. Why, why, why echoes through my prayers when I touch on certain details, but there are other things that have come into my life in the midst of the chaos and confusion that I can see clearly. The fruit was fertilised by this particular story. I pray that I won't confuse the events of my life with God manipulating my life. I pray that I'll continue in a passionate pursuit of truth and celebrate the fruit that God grows along the way.

I pray that I'll be content with my loose ends.

Loose Ends

This book doesn't have symmetry
Like this poem doesn't have rhyme

Wouldn't it be better to wrap up the story with a pretty bow?
This is the story of my life that's still unfolding, though, so I can't tell you the storybook ending.

This book is a trajectory
A look at the past
And what led me to the present

With some hopes along the way

I don't know what happens when you turn the page, when I wake up tomorrow, when you go to sleep tonight.

My preferences are clear: I'd like to walk again.
When I wrote this poem, I was in a wheelchair.

Acknowledgements

This book was a long time in the making, and I'm grateful to Amanda and Ruby for giving it the final push to the best version it could be. Any mistakes left are mine, but the final pass through and cover design were my last hurdles that you both helped me with.

Huge thanks to Sarah, Michele, Alyson, Carol, Ellie, Paige, Ryan, Kay, Bekah, and Shirley for comments on the bulk of this text. I'm also grateful for Laurin, Jan, Sorche, GI, Bonnie, Bri, Nicki, Jennnnnnn, and Shirley who gave significant feedback on my initial draft six years ago. There were lots of others who read bits and pieces and encouraged me in different stages, and I'm grateful for all the positive input from so many others. Thank you especially to every student who let me tell a part of their story as it intersected with mine. Everyone named and a few alluded to have read and given consent for the inclusion in this memoir. To Maggie, Nick, Isabel, and Alyssa, I add special thanks for your help in how I was able to communicate the most vulnerable bits in this book.

www.ingramcontent.com/pod-product-compliance
Lightning Source LLC
Chambersburg PA
CBHW052141070526
44585CB00017B/1928